She's not for you.

By Kasim Power

ISBN# 978-0977122790

Acknowledgments

First, I'd like to thank God for giving me the gift and opportunity to write another book. Kimora and Bella never forget Daddy loves you Mom, Grandma my entire family there are so many names just know I love you all. I'd also like to thank my Wife Sloan for even putting up with me. Kevin, Bryon, what can I say but let's get it. Also, to my readers thanks for supporting True Brothers and their Pride and Joy as well as Hood Lover, Someone's Gotta Be on top, Year of the Gentlemen, and my upcoming novels Pure Evil, Caught between women. I can't wait to start the TV series. To my family and friends, and to everyone all the book clubs I hope you'll enjoy reading She's not for you, because I enjoyed writing this book. Also, Cousin David, Hope can't wait to work with you. Ms. Robinson, Jamie Hector, and Dominique, thanks for everything when I first came to Moving Mountains I was taking my screen writing courses. and now I've had 4 Productions, and directed and wrote and acted in them. For those that haven't read my third 3rd novel Someone's gotta be on top based on my stage play know that God is really good so let's keep moving those mountains. My brother Mookie know you are never forgotten, Antawn, Bolo, B- Rutland and everyone

out there keep pushing and going for your dreams. To my Advisor Wyatt, and Hope Clarke, thanks for putting up with me I think I get too you too more than I did my cousin David, back when he taught me too drive. Cousin John, Aunt Linda, Emma Again for those that didn't get to see any of my stage play's Someone's gotta be on top, She not for you, and my new on Mother Love say's Prayer changes things they'll be in Brooklyn 2018. To contact me you can email me
BlackpoweProductionrpublishing@gmail.com

Books by Kasim Power

True Brothers and their pride and joy, Hood Lover, Someone's gotta be on top, Year of the Gentlemen, Pure Evil.

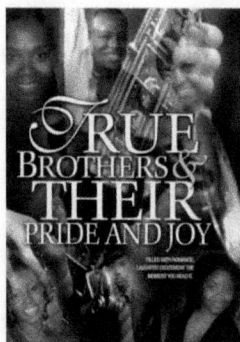

She's not for you.

Kasim Power

BLACK P✊WER

Publishing

1

Derrick

"I don't know Doc; I don't think I can open up to another woman. I mean all they want is either to know what you can do for them."   Money, Sex, or that Thug dude. A lot of them want.
"Well, Derrick do you think it's the kind of women you attract?"

"Oh, I attract some beautiful women Doc."

I never said you didn't, but there must be something you're doing wrong to not have kids or be married. I mean that is what you want right?"

"Yes, that's true. I want to be happily married and have a wife that's not about games. I mean women want a good man, and then when they get one, they don't know how to act. All of a sudden, they're confused because there not used to being treated right."

"Well, Derrick how do you know you're a good man?"

"Because I know, I treat my mom good I was raised right by her."

"Ok Derrick, I hear all that but how well do you know yourself? As a matter of fact, I'd like you to do an assessment of yourself. I think then you'll know who and when to commit yourself to."

"You know that's a good idea, I'm going to do just

that Doc."

Man, that Doctor Wave, had some big points I think. I'll start tonight. I texted my boy Carl letting him know I left the doctor's office. Carl and I been friends since we were kids but our vision on women was totally different. Carl, was always all over the place. One moment he'd be in love and if things got tough in the relationship he'd be out. He'd tell me he's tired of meeting women who are drama queens. I understood where he was coming from to a certain extent. This year things are going to be different and I was determined to see that they are. I'm going to make sure I put God first everyday, I'm not going to start something and not finish it. I'm differently going to be more verbal because I'm tired of having disappointments in relationships. So,

I'm going to actually do what Dr. Wave suggested. I texted Carl, letting him know to meet me at my mom's house.

30 minutes later at my mom's house, I was having a talk with her not about what Doctor Wave, and I spoke about but more about the holidays because Christmas was just 3 weeks away. I let mom know I was going to get myself a God-fearing, woman because I was tired of going from woman to woman, and I

think Carl was also, but he just didn't want to admit it.

"I'm proud of you son. Good for you." My mom said.

"Thanks, mom. You don't know how much that means to me."

"Well, you've got be true to your word. And God don't like you going back on your word. And these Women, out here their, just looking for good men like you and Carl, because there's so many of our black families being torn apart."

"Well that's why I want to be married first mom or engaged before I have a child." I said.

"Well that's the plan." Carl said as he walked inside the house.

"Yo, you don't just walk inside the house man."

"My bad Derrick, but the door was open. How are you Mother LOVE?" Carl asked giving my mom a kiss on the cheek.

"I'm fine Carl, and my door is always open. This is a house of piece, happiness, and it's a place where all are welcomed in the house of the Lord."

"Mother Love I have a confession to make."

"Go on ahead Carl, what's on your mind."

"You'll my find this funny or don't believe me. Because of the life style I used to live. But anyone can change if their willing too."

"Carl what are you talking about?" I asked.

"I'm just saying, I'm letting you both know I've decided to give my life to Jesus."

"Ha, ha, ha." I kept laughing.

"What's so funny? It's a problem giving my life to God?"

"Not at all Carl, I'm laughing cause, I just told Mother Love I'm doing the same thing."

"Now you boys must be aware once you give your life to Jesus there's no turning back. Psalms : 37:5 and 6 Commit your way to the Lord. Trust in him and he will do this. He will make your righteous reward shine like the dawn your vindication like "the noonday sun.""

"We're ready to commit." We both said.

"I'm proud of both of you." Mother Love said.

"God is good." I said.

"All the time." Mother Love said.

"Mom if you'll excuse me and Carl we have some things to discuss."

"We do?"

"Yes, we do. Now let's go."

When we left my moms, house and went into Carl's Chrysler 300. I looked at him and shook my head.

"Ok, Derrick, what's on your mind?"

"Megan, that's what, and also you."

"Me?"

"Yes Carl, have you been baptized? And the reason I asked cause, I want to make sure you ready for this road you about to go down."

"What the hell are you talking about Derrick?"

"I'm talking about what you said to me and Mother Love back there about getting right with God."

"I am ready for that. And I don't have to be baptized again I was when I was a baby."

"Brother, you were just talking about being reborn."

"Yes, I said I was getting right with God Derrick what's your point? Look don't go Judging me."

"That's not what I'm doing."

"Then what are you saying Derrick?"

"What I was going to say to you is, I'm going to tell Megan I'm getting baptized, and that I'm going to be celebite until I'm married."

"You gone, give up pussy? And wait until you married?"

"Yes, it's what I want Carl.

"I'm not knocking you Derrick. I'm just saying you're a better man than me because even the best of men are sinners."

"We're all sinners, but remember in Hebrews 13:4 when they talked about how marriage should be and how a bed should be kept pure."

"Yeah so."

"So that's how I want things with Megan."

"Oh, and you think she'll accept that?"

"Of course, why wouldn't she?"

"I'm just saying not many people follow all God commands. That's where we fall short at."

"I hear you Carl, look I'm going to meet Megan now." I said giving him a five goodbye.

I was hoping Carl would come. But this is something I have deal with on my own.

2

Carl

I love Derrick like a brother, but sometimes he can be unrealistic. Today's women are not like they are when our parents or grandparents were young. Same with some brothers, but I'm not going to be a man that complains, because Gods got a plan for me. I was on my way to see my lady Rachel, we've been seeing each other almost a year now. And I'm in love, man I'm really in love. Did I mention I'm in love, I could see Rachel and I having our first child together, we talked about it for a while now and at first, I wasn't ready at all. I just started my new job with Real Creations, as one of their models. I was happy that Stefan got his company back and how well the company was doing. I even helped Rachel get a job as a model here. We met each other through the man I call my Uncle. 30 minutes later I was at Rachel's apartment and after explaining thinking. Rachel took me for a joke.
everything to her and telling her what I was

"I will get closer to God you just watch."

"Babe, I'm not saying you can't, but what I am saying is I don't think you're ready for all that commitment. I mean all the meditating and praying can you really stick to all that?"

"I can and I will just watch."

"So, let me put this pussy on you, daddy because I know you love it juicy." She whispered in my ear.

Rachel, stared at me and started doing tricks with her tongue as she grabbed my manhood, and started rubbing on it. Words couldn't explain how much I was in love with Rachel and this is why I said to Derrick he was fooling himself. I moved in pulling Rachel close to me and she turned me around and threw me on her bed. Immediately unbuckling my belt and paints going to work and as she licked my balls and went on handling her business. Within seconds I was naked and ready for what Rachel, had to offer me. My lady was a very sexy woman.

"Hold on honey the doorbell."

"Can't that wait babe?"

"I'll be right back babe. Remember we talked about spicing things up in the bedroom."

"Yeah, I remember us talking about it."

"Ok, so just keep your eyes closed."

I did as I was asked and I had no idea what Rachel had in mind but I was glad she took into consideration what I mentioned. The doorbell rang again and Rachel went to answer it. I kept my eyes closed and when Rachel came back in the bedroom I still had them closed.

"Can I open my eyes now?"

"No, not yet honey." Rachel said holding my manhood.

I smiled as Rachel kissed me. "Ok, honey you can open them now."

"Rachel what the fuck is going on?"

"Dude get the fuck off, of me." I shouted out.

"Carl what's the matter with you? We talked about spicing things up."

"Not with no next man, I'm not gay." I jumped and threw a right hand, lead punch at him which connected to his jaw.

"Carl, stop now please."

I wasn't listening at all I kept throwing punches that connected but he ducked my 4th punch and punched me the ribs and then punched me in my noise. "Rachel, you told me you both talked about this."

"Adam stop! We did speak about this."

My noise was bleeding and I looked at both of them, as I got up off the floor. "Rachel, your sick bitch you should know I'd never agree to this bullshit."

"You men are damn cowards, you want a woman to have a threesome with you so badly, and when she brings another man to the bedroom to have a threesome it's a problem."

"Bitch don't you get it. I told you I was doing right by God.

"Read your damn bible Leviticus 18:22 It's a damn sin for a man to sleep with another man and same for a woman."

Wham!

I was punched in the stomach again by this guy. "You'll have plenty of time to think about it behind bars. I'm placing you under arrest."

"What? I said holding my stomach. The guy pulled out his badge and read me my rights I can't believe Rachel, just stood there and watch.

"I warned you about your temper plenty of times Carl." Rachel said kissing Adam.

"You're going in for assaulting an off- duty officer."

After putting handcuffs on me Adam immediately read me my rights. I watched Rachel just shack her head and this was a woman I was in love with.

20 minutes later at the percent

 "Well Mr. Carl Powell it appears there's a warrant out for your arrest. You see God don't like ugly." Adam said.

"What the hell are you talking about?" I said.

"You never arrived in court when you were supposed to."

"What?" I said looking confused.

"Yeah, it says here you were supposed to be in court and you got arrested for having prostitutes. And you call yourself a man of God?"

"Look I've, left that life style alone!" I shouted out. "Then why didn't you appear in court. It doesn't even matter because you about to do some time now. And I'm about to do this damn paper work."

"Don't I get to make a call?"

"Yeah, soon as the sergeant says s you can."

Minutes later I was able to make my call and so, I called the one person I knew who would understand that everyone has a pass. He knew I was changing my life around.

"Hello?"

I paused for a moment. I usually wasn't one to hold back but suddenly I was thinking this wasn't a good idea. "Hell...Hello."

"Carl? Carl is that you?"

"Yes, look I need you to bail me out of..."

"Of jail, consider it done nephew."

"What? Thanks Uncle."

"That's Deacon to you."

"Yes, ok just get me out of here please."

"I said consider it done. Now let's go ladies, somethings come up."

30 minutes later.

"Oh, man God is good. Deacon was right there with a suit case and I watched him hand my bail money to

"How the hell did you know what percent I was in? It's as if you knew I got arrested."

"I did know you got arrested now let's get you out of here nephew."

Once outside. "What the hell were you thinking? How many times have I told you and Derrick you can't change a ho, into house wife. You can't make a woman be someone she's not cut out to be. All you can do is pray for them."

"Uncle Leroy."

"That's Deacon Leroy to you. And you're lucky the sergeant owes me a favor now we just have to wait for your court date.

"Ok Deacon Leroy. How the hell did you know I was arrested?"

"Rachel told me. Did you forget she used to work for me? See she put it on you so much you forgot how you met her. "But Deacon."

"You forgot what she is about? You forgot I used to tell you and Derrick you can't treat all these women out here like a wife, until she is your wife because not every woman is wife material."

It made no sense arguing with Deacon Leroy. Besides he did pay my bail 10,000 and all I could do was listen to what he was saying. Not everyone knew about his transition he made a while ago. As much as I didn't feel like hearing what he was saying I had no choice.

"Now nephew do you remember when Jesus took Peter, James and John up the mountain and told them not to tell anyone what they saw?"

"Yes, I remember reading it."

"But do you understand it? Because I don't want you not to believe, because they didn't believe Jesus, until they saw Moses and Elijah with their own sad eyes."

"What's you point Uncle Leroy?"

"That's Deacon."

"Ok Deacon Leroy what's you point?

"My point is a lot of people are not going to believe you've changed until you show them."

"Excuse me and what about you?"

"That goes for me also only some believe. But God is working on all of us, so Carl, remember you've got to be patient and know Gods got a plan for all of us.

3

Gabrielle

This can't be my life, it just can't be I'm going to tell him I want out and I need a change. The only question is will he be willing to accept that I no longer want to live like this. It was almost 2:00 am and I was waiting for him to come to my house. He texted me saying he had something to take care off before he saw me, God give me strength. In the past I'd be excited because I needed the money and I know he always cared for his employees. He wasn't hard on me like he was the others and over these past few months I'd seen a change in him. He told me ever since he found his daughter, he had a change of heart on how he did business, but he could never let people know he had grown a soft heart. I understood because a lot of people would easily use that to their advantage. I wasn't brought up like that I had kind of a rough life, because my teenager, and I was forced to live with my dad mom died of a drug overdose when I was a when I was 11. He did his best on raising me and although he remarried when I was 12 by the time I was 16 he was locked up because of a crime. I understood and as for my stepmom I had lost all respect for her. My father went to jail and died because of that bitch Gloria, one night my father came from work only to catch his wife in bed with another man. My dad did what any person would have done in that situation which is kick, both their asses. The only thing charges were pressed against my father and he was put in jail, but my father Charles died a proud man. Life got hard for me when my dad was in prison I'd been living on the street, because I was kicked out the house by Gloria and her new man Clint. Now I'm 21 and I'm ready for a really big change in my life. It's just time to let my employer know I'm not going to be about this life anymore. Just a few hours ago I was raped at gun point and I had no one there for me no one to turn too. I asked God, how can he allow this to happen and how can he allow such cruel people to do this? I filled out a police report, but that's all it was, was a report.   Describing the man who did this was not going to be enough for me.

I even let them know I managed to get the gun from the man as he put it down wanting to fuck me Doggy style.

I grabbed the gun and shot right at him. I missed but he managed to yank the gun from me and as every muscle in my body tensed. He ran off but not before hitting me with the gun. I put in the police report. I want vengeance and somehow, I'm going to get my revenge.

My cell phone rang I already knew it was, he had a special ring tone. "Hey! I'm here."

"Ok just give me one minute." I said as I opened the door.

"Now what the hell happened to you? Because I didn't like how you were sounding over the phone."

I blinked and as I picked my head up I came face to face with the man that's been like a father to me since I met him. Moments later after explaining to him what happened and how I felt he hugged me and told me he understood.

"Now that I'm at a new place in my life God, has put some new kind of love in my heart."

"Leroy, are you all right?"

"That's Deacon Leroy, to you. And of course, I'm alright. Now that I know why you haven't been alright I have something to say to you."

"And what's that. Because I just made it clear I'm not living that kind of life style anymore."

"Of course, you're not. So, I'm going to say to youyou're a strong woman. Don't ever forget that."

"I don't feel like one. Vengeance will be mine!"
I shouted out.

"Peter, once said do not reply evil with evil or insult with insult. We should reply evil with blessing, because to this you were called you were called so that you my inherit a blessing."

"Thank you, Uncle Leroy."

That's Deacon Leroy. Also, when you learn the words in the bible and what they mean you'll understand life a lot better."

"Excuse me?"

"Proverbs 6:24-26, 24. to preserve you from the evil woman, from the smooth tongue of the adulteress. Do not desire her beauty in your heart, and do not let her capture you with her eyelashes; for the price of a prostitute is only a loaf of bread, but a married woman hunts down a precious life."

"What are you saying Leroy? Excuse me Deacon Leroy."

"Thank you, now what I'm saying is you deserve to be a wife and right now you are ready to have a great life. Amen"

"Amen."

I smiled and hugged Deacon Leroy, although I didn't know he even became a Deacon, but that explains the sudden change in him.

"So, you told me you're ready for a change in life. No more stripping, you want out the game completely?"

"Yes, I do."

"Then come to my office."

"Excuse me?" I hope he didn't think I was going to fuck him to get out this type of life style.

"What I'm saying is come and get baptized and come to bible study. It'll be good for your spirit and soul, sister Gabrielle.

4

Mother Love

Next day Sunday 3:00 pm

"Son bitterness can keep you from your destiny and the life God has for you."

"Ma, why are you telling me this?"

"Because, I need you to let go of things you don't understand. Always keep your heart pure. It takes a lot of discipline and practice to brush things off."

"I hear you Mother Love."

"But, are you understanding what I'm saying? Because bitterness takes energy, God has a purpose for you."

"And what's that?"

"I don't know, but I do know is what God has planned for you, it can't be stopped by people."

My son Derrick came over and gave me a hug. Derrick and I have a great mother and son relationship. Whenever I need to tell him something straight I'd do it. It was up to him to listen and follow through with what I'd say. He told me the breakup Carl and Rachel had and how my brother had to bail him out.

"You both need, to just live life and laugh it's good for your souls."

The doorbell rang and my son looked at me smiling before going to answer the doorbell. As he went to answer the door I noticed my son Derrick is becoming more and more wiser that's God's doing. I just sat there on my couch holding my Bible and thinking what a might God we serve. All people have to do is allow God to enter their hearts and have faith in his ability. I have to admit there was a time I was angry at God and couldn't understand why I was going through what I went through before I became the woman I am today. I'm known to everyone that knows me as Mother Love. 2

Years ago, when my husband Derrick's father passed I found out he had five mistress. Or whatever these young people call these types of women. My husband died in his sleep next to me but at the Wake and funeral, I wanted answers. I found out he been helping women, as well as people in the community without me, even knowing. These weren't even women he was fucking, some were just married women who he helped get their marriage back on track. And they were women he was helping with their financial problem. I was approached by Debra, one of the five women who came to the wake she told me my husband, helped her and her daughters get into a shelter. I ask her why didn't she just get help on her own. But I was told my husband said God put it in his heart to be her helper and that's what he did. Don't get me wrong. I wasn't jealous but I was curious as to why I never knew this. The majority of these women went to our Church at St. Anthony's. I'm no fool though. I know these Jezebel heifer's, was probably trying to weasel their way in my home or into my husband. I was confident my husband would never commit adultery but if he did he's got a date with God on that one.

I was just upset that I never knew about this. These past 2 years I've made it my business to continue what my husband started. It took a while but I had finally forgiving myself for all those times I accused my husband for committing adultery. I never had proof of my husband not being faithful so I accepted he died I faithful man and started Bible study in my home every Sunday and Wednesday. I always felt a big relief these past 2 years and understood that my husband Charles had his own reasons for not telling me why he started helping the community without telling me. Only God can dictate a person's real enemies and know what's in people's hearts. For now, I was about to welcome my brother Deacon Leroy who I'm proud of only time will tell how much he's into God, although I'm not one to Judge and I just pray that my son, Brother, and Carl learn to have faith and trust God like I have.

5

Derrick

60 minutes later.
"You know Derrick, you say the nicest things, but your timing is always off."

I arrived at Megan's house ready to have a talk with her but Megan had other things on her mind. She was in a sexy black nightgown and I had to admit what Megan was wearing was exposing her big Melon's. Megan knew I'm a breast man God help me, I've got to be strong. Megan   , came kissing on me. "I love you, Derrick."

"I love you too Megan, which is why we need to talk before you start something that I'm going to have to finish."

"Then finish it, babe."

Now usually Megan wouldn't even have to ask me to finish but it's a new year and I'm a changed man.

Meagan kept kissing me and whispering in my ear. "You ok babe? Oh, you want me to go down on you?"

"No Megan, now can we talk please?"

Megan immediately got up off her knees. "Ok, Derrick what is so important that you have to tell me?"

"I'm not just about having sexing in a relationship."

"Excuse me?'

"What I'm saying is I've been changed. I'm celebite I've been baptized again, and I won't be having any more sex until we're married."

"Repeat that!" Megan said.

Megan gave me a look I'd never seen in her. I smiled at her explaining to her the transition I was making.

Megan wasn't too happy with what I was saying at all. "Mother fucker, you had me get dressed up, and looking sexy for your ass and you telling me now you're celibate. Derrick, what the hell has gotten into you?"

"1st of all I didn't make you do anything. Second, that was your choice to surprise me. 3rd I want to do right by God."

"Get out just get the hell out of here!" Megan shouted.

"Are you serious?" I asked.

"That's something you need to ask yourself."

Now that was the nail in the coffin because no one is going to question my commitment to God. I just walked out of Megan's house and texted Carl telling him to meet me at the Kings Theatre.

I love Megan, yes, we'd have our arguments here and there just like any couple, but we always worked it out. Now that she just kicked me out her house because I'm not giving my body to her, because I want to do right by God it's a problem.

I'm not knocking other people who chose not to be celibate but Megan, who again I'll say I love I expected her full support on my decision. I expected her to join me in this celibacy. My heart might have wanted want Megan wanted but my wisdom and knowledge that I'm gaining knew better. I guess temptation took over her emotions because I'm a man of God and I intend to do my best and stick to my word.

2 hours later

I stepped out the Uber car I was in front of the Kings theatre Carl and I had just broken up with our ladies and we both needed something to take our minds of our breakups. I suggested we go and see the All-star comedy jam. I believed in what my mom said about Carl and I needing Live, and laugh, but now we had no women in our personal lives to love. "Hey, there you are man. You're late." Carl said.

"Let's not forget you're getting a free ticket Carl and that's only because things with Me, and Megan didn't work out."

"So, I'm your rebound?"

"Whatever, wow, wow."

These two brown skin sisters who gave their tickets just got both of our attention. They walked inside looking sexy but immediately Carl cut them off.

"Excuse me, ladies, this can be a beautiful night if we go a double date."

"And how's that we don't even know you."

"My names Carl, and this is Derrick, coming. We're both men of God and it would be a crime and punishment if you don't let us take you both out."

"A man of God I like the sound of that why don't you tell me more about yourself Carl. My names Keisha and this is Gabrielle." Keisha said.

I looked at Gabrielle as we exchanged a ticket each and before I knew it Carl and I was on a double date.

Hello Gabrielle, my names Derrick." I said extended my hand.

My names Gab… I mean Gabrielle, I'm sorry I'm just a little nervous I was listening to your friend Carl when he said you both are men of God."

"Well he wasn't lying about that but right now let's enjoy ourselves because even Jesus say's laughter is good for you."

"And why would you say that?"

"In Luke 15:10 when a person gives their life to Jesus the angels in heaven start smiling and feel a great joy. That's why I said laughter is good for you."

In that case, let's head inside.

We both gave our tickets and headed inside ready to get our laugh on.

While we were in our sets we both watched Smokey Suarez hosting it. The All-star Valentine comedy show.

When the show was over Gabrielle and I went to go meet Carl and Keisha but they had other plans we saw them headed in a car with Keisha driving off.

"That damn heifer! How dare she!"

"Hey Gabrielle, I can get us an Uber to take you home it's not a problem."

"And what you think you gone come to my house and fuck me. I'm flattered and all, and the flirting you and your boy was doing."

"Woo, woo, woo, timeout slow down sister. I'm not that type of guy. I said pulling out my phone and pulling up the Uber app.

I immediately put what Gabrielle just said out my mind so I can concentrate. Damn as fine as Gabrielle is that was just a turn-off but God has taught me to make sure I'm safe and those that are in my presents are safe.

"I'm sorry about that Derrick but I'm..."

"Hey, Gab, girl you ready to come get this paper we going to this club by the broadway junction."

"No, I'm not about that life anymore. Besides my man wouldn't like that."

"What life is that? I asked.

"It's nothing Derrick as I said I'm sorry about that it's just that shit Keisha did well was fucked up but why the interest in me getting home safe?"

"Well, I'm a man of God."

"We all are children of God, don't try to run game on me."

"That's not even where my mind is sister. You see Psalms 4:8 In peace I will lie down and sleep, for you alone, LORD, make me dwell in safety." I said to Gabrielle.

I looked at her with a straight face and she stared at me smiling. I was wondering what was going through this woman's mind.

"Ok, so you know a bible quote big deal."

"It's about keeping you safe, that's important Gabrielle."

I kept my cool as the Uber car arrived and went to open the car door for Gabrielle and kept my cool but I was wondering would I get a serious conversation out of her if I opened up and told her I was celibate or did I just make a huge embarrassing mistake? Only God knew the answer to that.

6

Gabrielle

"So, what's your favorite fragrance?
"White Diamond."

"Ok cool, mines is Jay-Z's 99."

"What's your vision of love as far as a relationship?"

"Excuse me?"

"I mean how do you receive love, Gabrielle?"

"And why are you so curious about that?"

"Well curiosity can lead to great things don't you think?"

"I do and they can be things you're not ready for." I said smiling and putting my head down.

I picked my head right back up and looked at Derrick this man is being honest and asking me these questions I just might have him come upstairs and put it on him. But I knew better and I was not going to do that and end up losing his respect. My old boss once said most men won't respect you if you give yourself up to him on the 1st night. Especially if you'll don't even know each other because most men only want the relationship without the title it's 2018 and I'm about change in my life. We were quit for about 5 minutes I we were both trying to think of something to say. Now we found ourselves in front of my place.

I don't know about you Derrick but I have rules. I

have respect for myself and I won't allow no man to be disrespectful to me. "Wow, wow Gabe slow down sister I said I was just making sure you get home safe. I'll leave now ok."

"No, no you don't have to Derrick. It's just that I'm a little nervous."

"Nervous? You don't have to be nervous look why don't we just watch a movie or something? And about those rules, we can make our own rules up as we go along."

I like the fact that Derrick was being honest and that he was being a gentleman as well. I took Derrick up on his offer and we headed to my place and I smiled because it might be great having company.

I opened up my door as let Derrick inside.

"Nice place you have here."

"It's not much but I try to manage. So, what are your expectation, Derrick?" I was still curious and knew to keep my guard up.

"To be honest I have no expectation, Gabrielle. I just want you to enjoy my company that's all."

"You're a sweetheart Derrick why don't you tell me about yourself while we watch this movie."

I put on Netflix and we both watched the man in 3b. Derrick touched my hand and it made me a little nervous but I gently smiled.

Well, my names Derrick Powell and I'm the only child about me I'm a celibate man I grew up."

"Wait, wait, hold up, your celibate?"

"Yes, I am. I wasn't always celibate but I'm doing things differently now."

'God this has to be your doing.' I said to myself.

As we continued to watch the movie Derrick went on to tell me about his life and what made him become celibate. I had to pee but I tried to hold it because I wanted to keep hearing what Derrick was saying because this man isn't a bad conversationalist at all. I like the fact that he was being honest and looking me in the eye. Because God knows I hate being lied too. "Excuse me a moment Derrick. I said as I went to the bathroom."

The doorbell rang. "Derrick, can you answer that please?"

I watched Derrick open the door as I was drying my hands off and this was not the type of company I was expecting. I came face to face with a couple of people I was not in no mood at all to be dealing with. "What can I do for you, Detective?"

"Detective?" Derrick said.

"Yes, my names Detective Williams. I'm here to ask your friend here some questions."

"And what might that be Detective?"

"We'll be the one asking the questions here are we clear?" Another officer came inside and said.

His voice scared the shit out of me but I tried my best to keep my cool because I didn't want to show any signs of weakness in front of Derrick. Derrick immediately positioned himself in front of me and looked at the Detective. "Please Detective, if this is about the parking tickets I owed, just know I've paid that off already. I already went to court and listened to what the Judge had to say. So why you here bothering me?"

Detective Black laughed at Derrick. First of all, I'm not here for you. I'm glad that you paid you ticket off.

"Of course, that's how NYC make their money."

"Ok, then why are you here?"

I know I was looking scared but hearing Derrick I no longer was now that he was standing up for me and I was glad this man was here to be by my side.

"Look I'm sorry if I caught you off guard, but I have a job to do and I intend to do it."

"Then why are you here?" Derrick said as his tone was louder.

"First of all, you'd better lower your voice. Second just relax because I'm here to tell your lady we've found the man who raped her."

'Omg after all these years.' "Good I hope his ass stays in jail for a very long time."

"It's not that simple Ms. You see Warren style is dead and your one of the suspects."

"What? Impossible!" Derrick shouted out.

"Son, I'm here to get to the bottom of his murder."

"Detective I think you better come inside." I said.

I didn't have to ask the Detective twice and he looked right at me and Derrick as he walked inside and looked at me and Derrick.

"So, Ms. Why don't you tell me where you were last night and what you were doing?" Detective Williams asked me looking right in my face.

7

Carl

I stepped off the elevator with Keisha, and as we walked toward her apartment. I looked at the time and saw it was after 1:00 am Keisha, and I had just met each other a few hours ago at the Kings Theatre. On our way to her place, we were joking and getting to know each other while we were in the Uber car on our way to her place. 20 minutes later after eating some chicken Keisha put in the oven and have a few drinks. Keisha and I were kissing on each other. She could really kiss and her lips were juicy and once our tongues touched one "Wait, wait." Keisha said.   another I could sense Keisha was ready to go there.

"What the matter? Did I do something wrong."

"No, no, Carl let me go shower that's all. A woman loves smelling fresh before getting her freak on."

I had to respect her and that's what I like in a woman. I love a woman who respects herself. While Keisha went to shower I got on my knees and prayed. "Dear God, I'm coming to you asking for you to forgive me and understand I'm trying to be a better Christian and forgive me for not being where Derrick is at I'm not strong enough yet father. I'm not celibate father I'm looking for that special woman and I'm hoping Keisha is her. I'm just looking for a woman who what to get close to you just like I do. I'm coming to you asking for more wisdom and knowledge and know this God I'm tired of pleasing the flesh God I really want to get close to you. Please help me in Jesus name Amen."

"Amen." Keisha said.

Keisha came out in a pink night gown and was looking sexy as hell. I put my hand over my face and just kept looking at her. She sat on her sofa smiling. So I'm dealing with a man of God?"

"We're all children of God Keisha." I said.

I wasn't sure how much of my prayer Keisha heard but I sure as hell wasn't ashamed to let her know what I'm about. "Look are you even a Christian? Because I'm not..."

"Excuse me, Negro, don't you dare come in my house and try to Judge me. And for the record I'm Baptist, you have a problem with that? The door is right there."

"Woo, woo claim down Keisha. Claim down, I'm sorry but I just want to be sure I'm with a woman whose heart is as precious as mine." I said as I pushed myself in front of her.

"So, what are you going to do? Because I'm fucking horny and..."

Before Keisha could say another word I put my tongue right in Keisha's, mouth. We were French kissing each other and Keisha immediately put one of my hands on her breast and the other on my penis. Within second my pants were unzipped and I watched Keisha go to work licking my penis and sucking it. I held her head and then stopped her because I wanted Keisha to know how much I respected her. "Are you crazy?" Keisha asked.

"Carl, I understand you're a Christian and all but don't ever stop me because I'm not gone stop you. Trust me God understands and remember he's a forgiving God."

This time we were in her bedroom and our tongues were locked to one another and I put two fingers inside her gently. I could tell her pussy was really tight and that's how I love it. I was kissing her neck as well and she kept moaning and holding me and her nails started to scratch my back. I love foreplay and I could tell Keisha was loving what I was doing. I decided I wanted to know her body I sucked her left breast and rubbed her right nipple gently. I looked at Keisha and she had a huge smile on her face. "You love that?" I asked.

"Yes, I do, now put that dick inside me."

I did as I was asked and Keisha didn't care who heard her moaning. We switch position from missionary to doggy style to her ride me and when she came so did I. Keisha collapsed on my chest and feel asleep, the work she had put in just now damn. I don't know if it was the liquor or what but this woman had some skills. I couldn't wait for round 2 because that's when the main event would start then I'd be able to see if she could really hang.

Keisha, and I both feel asleep in each other's arms. This is one woman I really want to get to know. I could see us having more than just a sexual relationship. A few hours later we were both laying down and I looked at Keisha and as she opened her eyes I smiled at her. "Hey, how'd you sleep?" Forget how I slept?" "It's time for round two right now."

"Wait, wait I don't have any more condoms. I like you and all but..." "Look, Carl, I believe in safe sex also. I'm not a ho, I fucked you because I really like you and enjoyed our conversation. I also like that you're a man of God." Keisha, said as she pulled out some women condoms.

We went back to French kissing one another but before Keisha could put the woman condom on the doorbell rang. "Don't answer that." I suggested as I kept palming her ass.

"I'll be right back babe don't worry." Keisha, said as she got up out the bed.

I heard Keisha, ask who it was and heard her open the door. I was hoping whoever the hell it was would leave quickly so we can finish our round 2. As I got dressed I heard crying and opened the door just so I can really hear it and I really wish to God I didn't.

"Keisha, how the hell could he do this to me? All the damn things we did in the bedroom and outside of it. I was just in handcuffs while he was eating me girl."

"Than what's the problem? What did he do?"

"Girl he left me for a damn man. Not only that he gave me a fucking STD."

"What girl, get out of here. I'm your girlfriend, you know I'm here for you."

Damn, I wish I would have stayed and worked things out with Carl.
"What that's what your ex-name was describe him?"

I've heard enough, I put on my shirt and came out the room. "So, we having regrets Rachel? Now you realizing you fucked up?"

"Wait, wait, wait up Carl you know my girlfriend Rachel? You're the man she said broke her heart?"

"Excuse me? If me turning my life over to God and wanting to be a better man hurts your friend, and she'd better me lucky not killing anyone is in one of God's ten commandments because..."

"Negro, don't you even at like you a true Christian because we just fucked each other! And I asked you a question?"

"Hold on a second. Bitch you just fucked my ex, Carl? Keisha, how could you?"

"You damn right I fucked her, I did. I got mine!" I said holding my manhood letting this chick's, know I got mine."

"1st of all Rachel, I didn't know he was your ex. But as for you Carl..." "Keisha, I'm sorry about that statement I just made. But as for you Rachel, you already know how things went down with us. I got arrested because of your ass."

I just realized Keisha, didn't deserve that. Just seeing Rachel and remembering what had happened that night.

"Now Carl what did we talk about on our way here?" Keisha asked.

"We talked about forgiving those who have hurt us in the past."

Keisha was right, that was one of our discussion we had on our way here last night.

"Look, you two I'm sorry. Keisha, I came here for some comfort. Carl can we start over?" "Now Rachel, you my girl and all but you asking for a beat down. You know I would have never done that to you. This Adam dude who hurt you wasn't Carl. Also, understand Carl, is my man now and him and I are going to be spicing things up in the bedroom early. Remember that favor you owe me.

"Yes I do girl again I'm sorry." Rachel said.

Before I could blink Rachel, and Keisha was tonguing one another down. As they both went to the bedroom I followed them and as Keisha said I'm not fully there yet. I do however want to be closer to God so I'm hoping he can forgive me.

I was watching Rachel, go down on Keisha and Keisha used her finger telling me to come to her and before I knew it my penis was in her mouth. I must have hit the lottery, because my new lady was a super freak. Keisha was the kind I usually wouldn't take home to my mother or bring around Mother Love, but I just really pray God can forgive us both.

8

Keisha

This is going to be a great day and a great year for me and my new man Carl. I'm great full that I even met Carl, but I was not about to have him bring baggage into this new relationship. My girlfriend Rachel, used to date Carl but I didn't know that until last night and that was after I put in on Carl, already and cut these feelings I have for him. It's not just the feeling though, I enjoyed the conversation's we had with one another. That's what put a smile to my face and the fact that Carl was becoming a man of God my boss Uncle Leroy, would call people like that a baby Christians. I had to get up and pee and I realized Carl, wasn't in the bed anymore. I let Rachel, know Carl, was my man now. I knew how Rachel got down and she's a user, but she must have real feelings for this Adam guy to let Carl go, but I let her know Carl, and I have a title even though we had met a couple of h   ours before Rachel came unannounced.

"Good morning babe. Carl said kissing me on my neck."

"Good morning to you too boo."

"Hey, you'll." Rachel said as she came out the bathroom dressed.

"Carl give us a minute please." I said kissing him in front of her.

"Keisha, what's up?"

"Rachel, I know you came to talk to me yesterday, but I didn't know Carl was the ex you dumped for Adam."

"Keisha it's cool, just treat him right because…"

"Excuse me I don't need you to tell me how to treat know man."

I knew I had to make my point and get this Bitch up out of here. Because the last thing I wanted was to be arguing especially after the fun part of our night was over. I was feeling too damn good especially after getting laid and have Rachel, go down on me. Although I knew Rachel, and I needed us to talk now was not the time because as I said I know Rachel, and talking to her about her wanting Carl, back would lead to lies and then I'd be getting pissed off. And a bitch like me would be catching a case. I just stared at Rachel for a minute before saying anything.

"Keisha, look I understand Carl, is with you now. As I said just treat him right, but please don't let your guard down."

"Rachel, I know you came for comfort and I know you came because of Adam. I'm sorry he hurt you but as I stated Carl…"

"I know, I know, Keisha Carl is your man now. We cool and besides he's your problem now. I've got my own."

"And what might that be."

"Adam, kicked me out. He wanted me to be a housewife, and you already know we're bitch's about getting our own money."

Rachel, was right here and I are Gogeta's. We met one another while working for Uncle Leroy one night.

"I was going to ask can I crash here but it's cool. I've got some money saved up." Rachel said as she exited my crib.

I made my way to the bathroom and sat on the toilet. I felt relieved as I exhaled, when I was finished I looked in the mirror and started to wash my face and brush my teeth. I'm blessed with this pretty face and these double D's God has given me not to mention I've got the brains to go with it. Like Rachel said we're Gogeta's. I stepped out the bathroom confident as always and as I looked at Carl, he took a glance at me and looked a me silently before kissing me. "Hey, how about we take a trip to IHOP and get some break feast and tonight we'll go to City Island."

"Ok, you pay for break feast and I'll pay for dinner." I said looking at Carl smiling.

"No problem at all."

I knew most men only cared about getting between a woman's legs, but Carl just feels different and usually, I wouldn't follow my gut but this time I'm following it because God's got a plan for me and my new man. "Let's go." I said pointing my index finger telling Carl come in the shower with me.

While we were both in the shower and letting the water touch us Carl and I stared at one another. You clean?" I asked.

"What do you mean? Off course I'm clean are you clean?" He asked me.

I didn't smile at all but this is just something that feel right I wanted Carl inside me.

"Keisha, I like you a lot but I think we both need to get checked out first."

"I just went to the Doctor last week you can check the papers there in my living room. Now when's the last time you were checked out?"

"Right after Rachel and I broke up."

I was brought back to reality by Carl. And hearing him made me want him more. I love an honest man,

I glanced down at Carl as he looked at me I nodded my head and immediately put his dick inside me and as we made love to each other our tongues was locked to one another we both heard the doorbell ring.

"Who the hell is it now?"

"Babe, it can't be that important. Let me answer it anyway." I said.

I put my rob on and Carl came out in his boxers and a tank top. "Who is it?" I said.

The person didn't answer the door. "Babe just answer, it maybe Rachel forgot something."

"Are you Keisha Strong and I take, it you're Carl Powell?"

"Yes we are Keisha, is this one of your ex's because I don't do drama. I've getting away from that shit."

"Do you'll know Rachel Simons?"

"Yes, we do I said what happened to her?"

"My names Detective Bruce and this is my partner Detective Felicia Lock. You'll both know what happened that's all the evidence I needed. Book them now."

"Keisha Strong and Carl Powell you're both under arrest for raping Rachel Simons."

'What the fuck? This can't be happening owe God this cannot be happening. God, what have we done.'

9

Derrick

I hung up the phone on Uncle Leroy because I was too busy enjoying the kissing and pleasure I was getting from my lady Gabrielle. My mind was totally focused on the love making we were having with one another. I let Gabrielle know I was celibate and it didn't bother her at all because she let me know there's other ways to make love then just having sex. She told me our minds can connect to one another as well as us getting a spiritual connection. That was a complete turn on, I kept holding her hips as our kisses were becoming more intense by the second. "Derrick, I know what your belief is and I respect that a lot and I want you to know you're the only man I'm with."

Gabrielle went to kissing my neck and whispered in my ear. "I want you Derrick, but for now just hold me."

I did as I was told, since our very 1st conversation I knew this is one woman I'd be into.

My lady Gabrielle is special, special to me and as we just laid down listening to the music that started playing from her phone. Gabrielle got a phone call and pushed it right to voicemail, but I told her to answer it. She looked at me telling me she didn't recognize the number and I picked up her phone and dialed the number that had just called. Although we didn't want to be disturbed something just told me to answer it because Uncle Leroy kept calling. "Babe, go and check your phone and call back whoever it is, because if Uncle Leroy keeps calling it's got to be important."

"Hello, Uncle Leroy, what's so important that it can't wait?" I said on his voice mail.

Now isn't this something, Uncle Leroy kept calling me and now that I'm returning his call it's going straight to voicemail. I just looked at Gabrielle, and as she turned to face me she looked at me telling me Carl, and Keisha, got arrested. "What?"

"Yeah, Derrick, the damn bitch and your boy Carl got arrested." "What for? Your girl set my boy up or something? Because Carl is what some people call a baby Christian." I asked.

"Excuse me, Look, your boy Carl is…"

"Is what?"

"You know babe, it doesn't even matter because my friend bailed them out."
"So, they're alright?"

"I guest look, Derrick, I don't want other people to ruin what we have."

"I'd never let know one mess up what we have." I said.

I sprang to my feet and kissed my woman, I wanted to let her know how much she meant to me. I was aware our relationship is still fresh and new but Gabrielle was special to me. We laid there both saying to one another we wouldn't let anyone or anything come between us. Before I could blink Gabrielle's, tongue was in my mouth. She quickly started feeling my manhood and I welcomed her feeling me. I started feeling her breast and grabbed her ass. 'God forgive us.'

"Just this once." We both said.

"Babe, let's feel each other." Gabrielle said.

We both smiled at one another and our kisses was more intense. "Wait, Derrick you aren't joking, are you? Because we don't have to do this."

I grabbed Gabrielle by her waist and was kissing her neck as my fingers made their way inside her paints. Gabrielle started holding my penis and quickly went and got on her knees.

"Wait, wait, babe, I've got respect for you."
"I know you do Derrick, but don't stop me because I'm not going to stop you."

Special, that's the word that came to my mind and this moment right now that Gabrielle and I are sharing. What I wanted to make our 1st time being intermate. I picked her up and held her kissing her as she took her bra off and let her body be seen. Gabrielle was very sexy, and it my me smile.

"What's wrong Derrick?"

"I kept smiling. "It's just you've got the body off a Goddess, I can't help but smile."

"Oh, really? Which Goddess is that?"

"Aphrodite, and yes, I really mean it, now make love to me."

For the next 2 hours, I did as I was asked to do and make love to my lady who one day I will be calling my wife. Because I made a promise to God the next woman I sleep with I will make my wife.

10

Mother Love

2 days later.
"Carl, even Peter was falsely accused."

"But, Mother Love I been set up. We've been set up by that bitch Rachel, and she's going to pay so help me."

"Claim down Carl, you have to realize…" "Realize, nothing Mother Love that bitch Rachel, really messed with my life. Keisha and I just started seeing each other, damn I wish I never really met Rachel."

"All I want is peace in my life, and live with a special lady, have a family and do right by God." Wham!

"Ouch, what was that for?"

"I slapped you because. One your mouth is being disrespectful 2 you've cut me off when I was saying something important."

"Ok, Ok."

"Now, as I was saying to you. Even Peter was falsely accused, and because he believed in Christ, he knew those that falsely accused him would be put to shame."

Okay, Mother Love I get what you are saying, but I'm going to get even and come looking for Rachel."

"You will do no such thing Carl, I love you like a son, and so I'm going to treat you like one. You will kill Rachel with silence."

"What do you mean?"

"I mean enjoy your time with Keisha, she's the new woman in your life."

"I hear you Mother Love, I have to thank Uncle Leroy, for bailing us out and I just have to have a little faith in Christ so Keisha and I can get closer to him together as well as each other."

"Now that's what I like to hear."

I was happy to see Carl, faith becoming stronger even after going through a bad experience with Rachel.

My bother Leroy stepped in the living room smiling. It's great that you still have faith Carl because I want you and the new lady in your life to come watch me in action. Now, this is what I love to hear and see, my bother went from pimping women to preaching to them. Over the years I tolerated my brother. Even when we were younger I've seen the women he'd get and get just about all of them to doing whatever he wanted. Since God opened his eyes and brought his daughter to him, he's been a changed man. He's now a man that talks the word of God to people, and I'm proud of him. Not long ago my brother Leroy bailed Carl, and his new girlfriend

Keisha out of prison. It was all over the news of Carl and Keisha raping this girl Rachel.

"Carl I've got to say."

"No Uncle Leroy before you say anything Keisha's one of a kind. Keisha's made me feel good and."

"And nothing boy, you don't ever go all in the first night you meet a woman. Now you say you're trying to get closer to God. You say you want your faith to be stronger."

"I do."

"Well, it's got to be a lot stronger because now that word has been out on the street and news people in Church are going to look at you totally different. Carl, I need you to be claim and focused."

"He will Leroy, I have faith in him just like I did with you."
I watched Leroy and Carl, walk out my house and my son and his new woman entered.

"'Carl, are you alright?" Derrick asked.

Carl, just glanced at Derrick and this as he walked out with my brother Leroy. I can tell Carl, was still bothered of being arrested for something he didn't do. My son Derrick, came in the house with a guess.

"Who's this Derrick?"

"Mom, this is Gabrielle, but you can call her Aphrodite."

"And why is that?" I asked.

"Because she's full of love. And your son Mother Love is in love."

I looked at Gabrielle, who is a young beautiful woman, but I still am a mother 1st so I knew I'd be having a woman to woman talk with her. Like most women my son Derrick dated I can tell Gabrielle, felt she was in the drivers set with my son, but she doesn't realize my son is a true man of God.

Derrick, go make us something to eat and Gabrielle and I will have a talk.

"Talk about what?"

"It's ok Derrick, I've been waiting to get to know your mother."
"You can call me Mother Love sweetheart."

"Ok, I know when I'm outnumbered."

"Gabrielle, how familiar are you with the book of Jeremiah?"

"Jeremiah, in the bible?"

Yes, dear, so let me tell you now Gabrielle, my son deserves to have a wife. If you're not capable of that."

"Hold on now, Mother Love, I am very capable of being a wife to your son. Your son and I have something special. Now I understand this is our 1st time meeting but I care and am in love with your son."

"That's what I'd like to hear Gabrielle, with that being said I need to know are you still…"

"No, no, no. I am a much better woman now. I love myself more than ever and to answer your 1st question I'm familiar with the book of Jeremiah."

"So, you understand why I bought the book of Jeremiah up to you?"

"Not really."

"Gabrielle, in the book of Jeremiah 29:6. Men learn that when they find a wife to make children and to keep that faith going."

20 minutes later

Gabrielle smiled at me while Derrick came back in the living room bring us food.

Gabrielle, I can tell was full of excitement and love. I can see why my son is in love with her, but when it comes to marriage for these 2 only God knows if that's going to happen.

11

Uncle Leroy

"Uncle Leroy, why are we here?"
"For the last time that's deacon Leroy to you."

Carl and I just stepped off the elevator at Brookdale Hospital. We were accompanied by Carl's new woman Keisha. Keisha, who worked for me for a very long time. Now I've given my life to the Lord and I'm here to show Carl and Keisha why they should also. As we all walked down the hall we ran into Tisha, she's another young lady who use to work for me. Now she's a head nurse and I'm happy she's doing well for herself.

"Hey, girl it's been a while, how's everything?" Keisha asked.

Keisha, it has been a while and you see what I'm doing with myself."

"I'm here with my man Carl, and Deacon Leroy, wanted us to come here."

"Listen why don't you two ladies catch up Carl and I are going to make a stop right quick."

"Where too? You do know I hate smelling the disinfectant's in Hospital's right?"

"But you never heard Jesus complaining when he went to go help the sickness."

"But, I'm not Jesus Uncle… I mean Deacon Leroy."

"You don't have to be, my point was Jesus never took a day off when he was healing the sickness and disease's and spreading the word of God. Don't you remember Mathew 9:35?"

"I do but…"

"But nothing, come on in this office now."

"What?"

Before either of us could say another word we both saw Rachel come out the office. She just stared at Carl and rolled her eyes at me.

"Can you believe that heifer?"

"Carl, don't be surprised by anything. I was told she was here early to get herself checked out. I suggest you do the same."

"So why was that bitch leaving this Dr. Wave office?"

"Who knows, but Carl that's not why I brought you and Keisha here. I want you to see that being part of a Church and one of the leaders in it, you learn to tolerate a lot of things you normally wouldn't."

"I'm still not following."

"Just following me."

Carl, and I visited 2 old friends of mine that were in their last days. Both ladies were dying form something that till this day has not been cured. Cancer, when we entered Terry, and Diana's, room we both said prayers and despite these women condition they were glad to see us. They were glad to see someone outside of their family come visit them. I held both women by their hand and as their grip tighten I knew what God wanted me to tell all these women.

"You see Carl, if your lady Keisha is not going to support you on getting right with God and I'm sure she is. But if she isn't then she's not for you."

Uncle Leroy, you bailed us out of jail to bring us here? Really?" Carl whispered in my ear.

"Oh, you both don't have to worry about paying me back. You can pay me back by getting right with God." I whispered back in his ear.

We both stood in silence for a moment while both women looked at us. Keisha came in the room kissing Carl and as I looked at both women I couldn't help but be thankful for God bring us together. "People God has brought us together for a reason and he's given us the strength and wisdom to let these to ladies know they are not alone."

For the next 20 minutes, I was preaching the word of God and Carl and Keisha was standing by me. After I was done speaking I sat there quietly remembering the times I had with these too women. I remember trying to get them both to stop smoking so much even I cut down on the cigars. You can take the horse to the water but you can't make him drink it. Because the more I tried to get them too stop the heavier they were smoking. I'm not talking no ordinary cigarettes, but this was not the time to be judging that's not what I brought Carl and Keisha here for. There's no doubt in my mind Gods got a plan for everyone's life and I just hope and pray he can understand that I bought these two here for a reason. Only God, my sister, nephew and Carl and now Keisha knows about my transition of me being a Deacon.

Hopefully, us seeing these people will bring some joy to Carl, and Keisha, maybe just maybe they can forgive Rachel and see there's always people going through something worse.

12

Derrick

3 months later Gabrielle, and I had just come from our third doctor's appointment. We were headed to finally tell my mom the news. I just pray to God she can forgive us just like Gabrielle, and I prayed to God to forgive us for having a child before we're married. "You ready to do this?" I said to Gabrielle, as I leaned in and kissed her. I love the way my lady is smelling and the scent she has on Michelle Obama's, fragrance. Gabrielle knows how much I love her and how important it is that I want to be married. I love where our relationship is heading because now we're engaged. At first, I was shocked that she was pregnant, because of me being celibate but I had to rethink and remember that one night, Gabrielle, and I had made love. Last night was a reminder of that night. My woman is a freak for me in bed. Before the lights went out last night Gabrielle, looked in my eyes giving me easy access for what was about to come. The goodies below her waist, we gazed in each other's eyes and her breathing became heavier, but I let Gabrielle, no I was in control and for her to just relax. The way we looked at one another was pure love.

Gabrielle, straddled her legs around my waist and immediately our tongues connected. We were kissing one another like high school kids and once our kiss was broken I went straight for her breast and her nipples. They were so hard it's as if I told them stand up. Gabrielle, let me know how strong my arms felt and they were gentle as well, I was sucking her left breast as well as holding her right one in the palm of my hand. Our kisses became more and more intense as our tongues kept wrestling with one another. Our kisses last night was pure passion full of fire. Once I penetrated Gabrielle, it was as if our bodies had melted against one another. She let me know she felt me in her stomach and that's when I went harder and harder, and lifted her legs up to my shoulders but brought them back down. I told Gabrielle, I didn't want to hurt the baby and she said she was alright and just kept going. Making love to her like she never imagined and Gabrielle bit my ear when she had cum over and over again. We both buried our heads into the pillow and my lady kissed me telling me she hopes this never ends.

Present.

As we entered my moms house I told Gabrielle, to ease her nerves and relax. "That's easy for you to say. What if she doesn't like me? She's your mom." "But, you my dear can call me Mother Love. And we are all children of God and he wants us all to love one another."

"Hello Mother Love, my names…"

"Gabrielle, I know your name and Derrick did you hear anything from Carl?"

Yes, Mother Love and he said him and Keisha have been going back and forth to court."

"Well don't you think they need your support? I mean Carl is your best friend after all."

"Mom, there's a reason why I haven't been going to court with Carl, I been to busy going back and forth to the hospital. But I have been texting him and praying for him and Keisha."

"Yes, we both have Mother Love."

"Boy you've been sick and haven't told your mother?"

"Mom, I've been fine. It's Gabrielle whose been sick off and on. You see Mother Love your going to be a grandmother."
The look on Mother Loves face was devastating I can tell I disappointed her. My mind had been consumed on how was we were going to tell Mother Love, the news of her becoming a grandmother I didn't bother to think of nothing else.

"Derrick, you're going too be a father? Now you understand your going to have to be there for Gabrielle? As well as show compassion to your child."

"I've been there for Gabrielle, and I've been to all her doctor appointments."

"He has Mother Love. I can honestly say that Derrick is the Ultimate Gentlemen."

"That's the way I raised him and how far along are you child? And for Derrick to go against his beliefs."

"I'm four months."

"What?"

"Now mom it was one night."

"Boy that's all it takes is one time."

"This Jezebel!"

"Now Mother Love, mom, your out of line Gabrielle isn't even like that."

"Oh, she's not like Carl's girlfriend Keisha? You both have you've both gotten so pussy wimped you've forgotten your beliefs."

"Now Mother Love, don't forgot Carl and I are grown men." I said looking at my mom.

"And don't you forget. I know how women operate. Don't forget I been on this earth longer than you both. I know the games women play to get what they want."

"Excuse me! Now no disrespect to you   Mother Love but, having a baby is a gift and your son and I are in love."

"Look Gabrielle, I'm aware about giving birth is a gift. Now your going to tell me you haven't been trying to seduce my son?"

"No I haven't."

"Then why hasn't he been coming to church? You and Carl, just looke at the mess he's gotten himself into. Messing with these Jezebel's you'll are both lost men."

Now mom, this is your future daughter in law. She's not like these other women out here.

"Oh yeah that's what you said about Megan."

"Mother Love, I can assure you I'm not like no other woman your son has ever been with." "Oh yeah, prove it." Mother Love said picking up the bible and handing it to Gabrielle.

For the next half -hour we were sitting in the living room and smiles were all across Mother Loves face. Gabrielle, was the one putting smiles on Mother Loves face. My lady was telling Mother Love bible scriptures and letting my mom know she wanted to get closer to God. Just like Carl and myself.

"Now I admit to the both of you that. You'll caught me off guard with me being a GrandMother. I'm happy for the both of you. And congratulations. Now let's get some prayer up in here."

13

Gabrielle

5 months later.

It was time, time for me to bring my little girl into this word and Derrick and I cans tart our lives as parents. For the last 4 hours I was laying on the delivery table with Derrick holding my hand. Dr. Solitude came in the room with 3 other doctors saying to us it was time. They drugged me enough giving me. 1 hour later I was holding my daughter in my hand and I was so happy it was all over. The pain us women have to go through when having a baby. All the sickness we go through and pain for 9 to ten months. Because of Eve and Adam not listening to God. It's like a gift and a curse because us women are filled with emotions during pregnancy. But having a child is a gift from God as well and that's because he's a forgiving God.

13 hours later Derrick and I we're finally home. I was totally exposed and not to mention feeling like crap. Thank God I had the support of Mother Love and Uncle Leroy and my soon to be Husband Derrick there for me. It's a miracle that I'm still

alive after the pain that I was in. I was holding my baby and that's all that mattered to me. "We finally did it babe, after all that work."

I immediately put Rose in her baby crib and looked at Derrick. "We? What do you mean we? Derrick you only did one thing!"

"Excuse me?" Derrick said smiling.

"You heard me Derrick! You only did one thing. Have you forgotten I'm the one who carried her for 9 plus months. I'm the one who pushed her out and I' the one who's body is still in pain."

"Oh, me holding your legs wasn't work? And being working up in the middle of the night wasn't work? Also hearing you scream your damn child is kicking me and helping you through those nights wasn't work?"

"You're a man your supposed too Derrick."

"And I was so don't stand here saying you did all the work."

"Whatever!"

"You know I'm right, that's why you not say nothing."

"Look derrick I just had a baby, I'm tired and I need to rest."

"Well you do that babe, Carl and I are going to celebrate."

"What! You haven't even bonded with your child, and your talking about hanging out."

"Look, I'm a grown man, I don't have to explain myself to you. Besides this was planned."

"You still need to discuss it with me first. I'm your fiancée Derrick." I said as I went to hold our baby.

The doorbell had rang and as Derrick went to open it to see who it was. He stormed right out the door, right past Keisha.

"What's his problem?" Keisha asked.

"I don't know Keisha." "Well you know how some men act the age of their shoe sizes." Keisha said.

Don't pay him ant mind. Anyway, what's up?"
"I should be asking you that. You're the one who just came out the hospital, I mean you both just had a baby. Did you finally tell him?

"Hell no, are you crazy? He doesn't need to know about that." I said looking at Keisha as if she lost her mind.

"I understand it's your past, but you should have been told Derrick, I mean you both did just have a baby."

"Which is the reason why I'm not saying anything. I finally have a family."

I don't know why Keisha, didn't understand that. I'm finally really happy, and most of all I have a family of my own. Know more getting caught up with men who claim their single only to find out their married. This is one relationship I don't want anything to go going wrong.

"Gabrielle, I hear you girl. You don't want to lose your man or family I get that but you know Derrick isn't leaving his family."

"Look chill out Keisha! Your scaring me, my past is my past and besides Derrick's not the type to walk off."

"Then why did he just walk off? You never did tell me why he walked off."

That's because it's none of your business. Now what brought you by because I 'm tired and you don't have to go home Keisha but."

"But nothing, come on Gab, I'm your girl I'm only looking out for you. Besides I haven't even got a chance to bond with my grandchild yet."

"Alright, alright."

"I still think you should tell Derrick though."

"Ok, Dr. Phil, since you want to do this. Did you tell Carl that your."

"Yes, I did he even participated one time. What man would turn down a threesome. That's why you should comfort Derrick and tell him."

"No, and wait, isn't that what you both got arrested for? It was on the news."

"Look, the point I'm making is being honest with Carl, made our relationship stronger. That's why you should be up front with Derrick and tell him."

"Look it doesn't matter, because we have a child together." I said smiling. "Your right Keisha but."

"But nothing look, I'm going to check on my baby."

"Gab, what girl let me just ask you something." "What is it now Keisha?"

"Gab, how long have we known each other?"

"What?"

"How long have we known each other?"

"Since 2 grade, why?" I wanted to know where was she going with this?"

"Because I just wanted to know how much you trust me?"

"Keisha what the hell are you talking about? You no you can talk to me about anything."

"Yeah, but first let's have some drinks. Let's even make a toast to your new baby." Keisha said pulling out a bottle of E&J.

"Just say whatever you have to say. And what are you trying to get me drunk for because I have to get to my baby."

"Ok, well as I said it's Carl's, birthday coming up. And this year I want it to be special."

"Well what do you have in mind? And how is it benefitting me?"
Keisha, was looking nervous. Whatever it is she not too comfortable telling me. I watched Keisha take another shoot of E&J. As she poured my cup.

"Well, Gab I want you to have a Manajatwa with Carl and I."

I just looked at Keisha shaking my head.

"Well, Gab aren't you going to say anything?"

"Yeah, Bitch you done lost your mind. What the hell do I look like having sex with my man's best friend."

"Look Gab remember that favor you owe me?"

"Oh, so now you going to try and Blackmail me?

Where the hell is all this coming from?" I was really curious.

"It's nothing Gab, look I'm going to let you bound with your daughter."

"Ok, you take care." I said as we both hugged one another.

Keisha, really had some shit on her mind and Derrick had plans I wasn't even aware of. I was going to do some serious praying for her.

14

Carl

I pulled up out of my Infiniti in front of Half Court sports Bar in Crown Heights. No one knew Keisha had just brought this knew Infiniti 2017, she said to me what's hers is mine and what's mine is hers. These past few months have been rough on us and going back and forth to court was stressful on both of us. All because of that Gold-digger Rachel, but God's going to deal with her my lady Keisha, went to check on Gabrielle, and I was coming to Half-Court Bar to celebrate with my buddy Derrick who's a new father. I was very happy for Derrick and Gabrielle, it made me think of Keisha and I having a life together. We fell for each other quickly and although some people like Uncle Leroy might have thought we were moving a bit too fast I really didn't give a damn. Before I could take another sip of my drink Derrick walked inside and   came up to me at the bar table.

"My man Derrick, you're a father now congratulations man."

"Thanks Carl, thanks a lot I appreciate that."

"So, when you and Gabrielle going to make another one?"

"After you make your first, oh my bad you don't want to be tied down to one woman. Any way where's Uncle Leroy?"

"Who knows where he is, and you should understand why I'm going to break up with Keisha. Just look at what we been going through. I don't mind being single again."

"You really like playing this tough guy shit Carl."

"That's not it at all Derrick, I'm just about getting mine. You know how we use to do Derrick." "That's the key word Carl, use to. Sooner or later you'll realize that hour or two of fame is played out."

"Oh, really?"

"Well, more like five minutes for you."

"Funny man, you acting as though you ready to tie the knot down with Gabrielle."

We both looked at one another, I just wanted to see where his head is at because I wanted to see if he was really serious about Gabrielle. Even though they just had their first child together.

"Look Carl, I'm committed to Gabrielle, and what if I am ready to tie the knot down with her? I mean we did just have a child together."

"That don't mean you have to marry her. But hey more power to you. But how do you even know she's for you?"

"Keep being with Keisha and find out." "I'm still with Keisha, it's just that I need a time out. I mean you know the shit we been through. The Rachel situation."

"Carl, I get that. But what happened to going to God? I mean you and your lady are going to have your arguments and disagreements."

"I get that, but come on Derrick."

"Carl, look if there's no arguing or you having had one disagreement there something wrong. I mean you and I planned on coming here and Gabrielle wanted me to watch the baby and bond with her."

"You see man, that's what I don't want to go through."

"Whatever Carl, look one day God's going to point you in the right direction and find you a good woman if he hasn't already."

"Now why you have to put God in this?" I asked.

I couldn't believe Derrick was really going there.

"Carl, you really should think about taking women serious, I mean Keisha is a good woman." "Hell no, haven't you heard anything I said Derrick. Look at what Rachel put me through. I mean I can honestly say I've seen how spiteful these women of today can be."

"Just what are you getting at Carl?" "I'm taking about the things women put men through when their children are born. The shit people go through period when a child is born."

"Carl, every couple has it's challenges. So, what's your point?"

"My point is I'm not trying to go through that shit. I'm just trying to make sure you understand what you're getting yourself into, before you tie the knot down."

"Well it is a thought."

Now don't tell me you afraid to commit to Gabrielle, after just having a child with her?"
"No man, I love Gabrielle to death it's you who's afraid to commit."

"You exactly right, I'm not setting myself up to get hurt. So just remember your only having sex with one woman forever." I said to Derrick.

"Oh forever."

"I looked at Derrick. "Yes forever, ever."

"Well that's good because there's to many STD'S out here."

"Derrick, that's why they invented condoms."

"So what, God gave us a brain and we as men don't even use it. Now Carl, I'm telling you if."

If what Derrick?"

If you going to commit to Keisha, Carl I'm just saying you have to be responsible. I mean that's what women love."

"Look Derrick, I'm responsible it's just I'm not putting myself out there and get hurt again. Derrick you my boy I'm just looking out for you."

"And I appreciate that Carl, but what I'm trying to tell you it takes a strong man to show he's committed to his woman."

"I hear you. Derrick, and you're right."

"I know I'm right, so let me just add something else to that. It takes a real man to open up his heart to his lady instead of keeping shit to himself."

"Look, Derrick enough of this commitment shit. I'm single Because I want to be. When I find Mrs. Right you will know."

"Derrick and I just stared at each other. This commitment shit was really starting to annoy me.

 "Carl."

"What man?"

"I got you. Ha…ha…ha…"

Derrick and some of the other people including the bartender PJ was laughing. Until Derrick's phone was vibrating and I saw him pick it up to answer it.

"What happened? Duty calls?"

"Shut up Carl."

"That's exactly why I can't be tied down to one woman. Especially when she knows I'm hanging out. Gabrielle gone ruin everything.

"Chill out Carl. She only text me to tell me her moms and pops came over and are going to watch the baby.

"Oh, Let me guest so nowhere and Keisha gone come to Half- Court and chill with us.

"Yeah they are."

"Well they gone miss the first part of the show."

We both watched this new Artist Jeremiah. I couldn't have been more happier for Derrick, I could tell he was really happy I hope one day I can experience that. If I'm with Keisha or not.

15

Derrick

My woman Gabrielle, came in Half- Court bar with Keisha, looking sexy. She had on a black dress and I was just smiling because the by the time her and Keisha walked up to us   both Gabrielle and I were kissing one another.

 "Ok, you too ready to make baby number 2 already?"

"Shut up Carl!"

"Gab, don't pay him any attention. So, what brings you both to Half- Court bar? Babe, look I'm sorry about earlier, it's just."

"Derrick it's ok, I know how hard this pregnancy was for us and the emotional stress we both been through."

"She came cause, she has something important to tell you." Keisha said.

"Keisha!" Gabrielle said as she shoved Keisha.

"What's going on babe? Is there something I should know?" I asked.

"No babe, we're here to celebrate with you guys. So let's just get our drink on. Gabrielle said kissing me again.

"Now you both know good and well you can't hold your liquor. Carl said.

"Well we all know you're the male version of those women from the talk." Keisha said.

I could tell Carl and Keisha still had feeling for one another, but I wasn't a person to get involved in other peoples relationships.

"Excuse me? I'm not the one who threw up on new years, and I'm not the one who needed someone to hold me up."

"Now why you got to you there. That's why your ass single now."

CARL looked stunned to hear that statement by Keisha.

"Really? Well I'm loving it because I can be in and out whenever I want."

"Oh, really that's what you like being in and out of women."

"Yeah so what man doesn't?"

"Let me tell you something Negro, it's 2018 and us women will not be statistics."

"You tell him girl because I sure don't put up with that disrespectful shit. Isn't that right Derrick?" "Carl, don't put me in this conversation. Cause you know you ladies can't handle the truth." "That's ok Derrick it's all good because thanks to Steve Harvey's Act Like Lady think like a man book and his other book."

Gabrielle and Keisha looked at each other and shouted out.

"He blow you men up." Gabrielle said.

"He blow you men up." Keisha said.

"And now our eyes are wide open, we can tell if a man is really into us or just wanting to get some."

"You tell him girl." Gabrielle said.

"Ok, you ladies made you're point. Now let's finish our drinks."

"This is why they shouldn't be drinking with us. All they do is talk, talk, talk. Derrick can't you control your woman?"

Gabrielle immediately jumped in Carl's face. "Excuse me Carl, I'm not one of these brainless women you're use to being with. Keisha's the best thing you ever had.

"You really think so." Carl said raising an eyebrow and smiling.

"Don't try to play my girl, and I already know your use to brainless chicks Carl."

"And what's that suppose too mean?"

"It means Derrick knows I'm not to be disrespected. I'm his queen not his slave."

"You go girl." Keisha said smiling.

"Ok Scobby doo. Do you need some Scobby snacks to shut up?"

"Look, you gone stop trying to play me Carl." "Oh my bad Scobby Dee, but still no one asked you where you was at so just be quiet."

Both Carl and I started laughing. Gabrielle looked at the both of us. "What bab? Look it was funny. Why don't we go get you ladies drinks? and let's have a toast."
"No man come on."

I immediately grabbed Carl by the shoulder looking at him. "let's go Carl, cause if I don't get none tonight cause of your BS.

"You forgot you just had a baby Derrick?"

"That's not the point."

16
Keisha

While Carl and Derrick went to get us some more I decided to approach Gabrielle again but in a different way. Fuck it let me just come out with it. "Gabrielle, you ever think of what we talked about earlier?"

"Yeah, and chick you done lost your mind! You needs Jesus!"

"Oh no, you didn't go there, Gab? I'm not the one who needs to find herself."
"Find myself?
Find myself? Look Keisha I'm just not going for that ridiculous fantasy of yours."

Damn, this isn't going to be easy. I knew that from the first time I tried to come on to Gabrielle. I'm sure she just needed a little few more drinks and she'll give me the answer I want to here.

"Look, Gabrielle your sexy and I know I could get the temperature of your body to rise." I said holding her hand and touching her hair.

"Stop, Keisha."

"Is there a problem lady's?" Carl asked.

"Yeah, it was looking like you ladies we're in a heated argument." Derrick asked kissing Gabrielle.

"This is why they don't need any drinks in their system."

"Shut up Carl!" Both Gabrielle and I said.

"Look, this evening was going smoothly until you'll showed up. Why don't you'll act like adult's."

"I actually have to agree with Carl on that one."

That did it. This chick really acting like she so innocent. I raised a finger at Gabrielle. "Trick, don't you dare act like you don't have no skeletons in the closet."

"And you need to stay in the closet."

"Do you both realize, you'll are making Carl look good. His predictions about you'll not being able to

hold your liquor. Come On ladies, you both are actioning like Ghetto queens now chill out."
I took another sip of my drink.

"Listen, I'm not the one who just had a baby has a good man and keeping secrets from him."

"Time out, time out. Gabrielle what the hell is Keisha talking about?

"It obvious son, the baby isn't yours fam." Carl said.

"Not now Carl!"

"Come on Derrick clam down."

"No, I'm not claiming down. Understand, but I don't play that secret shit."

"Well Gab, spite it out. I told you tell him long time ago."

"Tell me what?" Derrick shouted out.

"It's obvious."

"Fine but I'm not the chick keeping secrets."

"Oh, it's time for world-star." Carl said pulling out his phone.

"Carl, I told you chill out. Now Gab, what the hell your friend talking about is that my daughter you had or not?

"Of course, she is why would you think differently?"

"Then what's with all these secrets I'm hearing about?"

"Fine before you and I got serious I was..."

"Was what?"

"Finally, this bitch has heart to tell her man the truth.
"Was....Was an exotic Dancer some people called it a stripper."

"What!" Both Carl and Derrick shouted out.

"That's why you use to work at night. Gab why didn't you just come to me?"

"Look you know my brothers doing time. I finally came out with it, but as I said I'm not the only one keeping secrets."

"Ok, what else is there Gab?

This was becoming real intense and if I knew things would get like this I would have kept myself and my mouth in the closet.

17

GABRIELLE

What was supposed to be a celebration turned out really ugly. I finally came out and told Derrick about my pass and although I tried my best to forget about it Keisha just made me relive it. But this Bitch spot is about to be blown up as well.

"Come on out with it Gabrielle. What the hell is Keisha talking about?"

"Fine as I was putting the baby to sleep earlier Keisha suggesting to me that me, you and her have a threesome.

"I'm down babe." Derrick said smiling.

"Excuse me, so you always wanted this slot? That's what you saying Derrick?"

"Hold up now, who you calling a slot."

"This why they shouldn't be drinking I warned you Derrick."

"Carl, man."

"What the truth hurts right?"

"So, Gab, who else you been giving head too with the Cookie while you were with me?"

I swung right away just missing Derrick's face. "Negro, how dare you."

"Don't even think about it."

"Derrick, wait man and claim down." Carl said grabbing Derrick by the shower.

Derrick, immediately punched Carl knocking him down. "Get off me, I swear that better be my Daughter."
Carl, got up off the floor looking at Derrick and boiled his fist immediately.

"Carl, are you ok?"

"Do I look ok? I just got sucker punched. I'd love for you to try that again."

"Carl, claim yourself down."

"Carl, I'm telling you. You got one more time to play yourself."

"Or what Derrick? What's really good?"

"I don't have time for this bullshit."
"Look man, everything was fine until they showed up. And Keisha you haven't learned from the Rachel situation?"

Keisha Walked up to Carl and me is crying. I didn't give a damn how this trick was feeling right now. My man, Derrick just stormed out of Half Court bar.

"Derrick wait, please wait."

"Gab, go get your man."

"I hope you're happy now Keisha? Because of you I might have lost my child's father." I said with tears in my eyes.

"I'm sorry I'm so sorry."

Sorry, that's what this bitch has to say to me. "Sorry, Keisha, sorry isn't bringing my man back to me sorry, isn't going to change the damage you've already done. As you can see there's no sigh of relief, if your ass just kept your freaky side between you and Carl none of this would have happened." I knew I had to go home and confront my man about this mess. Damn, some people are just jealous of other.

18

Mother Love

The next day.

I'm finally a grandmother, and proud of it. My son and Gabrielle, are engaged and I can't wait to meet my granddaughter. Although I had guest coming to day I was awaiting for Derrick to bring my grandbaby. Derrick walked inside my house without carrying my grandbaby. He wasn't even smiling, but I smiled at him as he kissed my forehead. "Well hello Derrick, you're finally a daddy congratulation's."

"Don't congratulate me."

"Boy don't tell me you done cheated on that girl while she was giving birth? Messing with one of those nurses."

"No, no, no it's nothing like that."

"Then talk boy, I've got Bible study to teach soon."

"I mean how could she do this to me? To us and our family."

"What are you talking about? Don't tell me you'll having disagreement after just having a baby together?"

"You just wouldn't understand Mother Love."

This must be serious. I expected my son to be full of smiles and have nothing happiness in his bones. "Derrick, why don't you tell me what's on you mind."

"As I said Mother Lover you wouldn't understand."

"Why don't you try me and find out."

"You're generation was the real generation for black folks."

"Boy stop with the riddles."

"How could she do this to me? It's as if I'm being punished I mean that's what it seems like."

Now I was getting a bit inpatient. Because I was looking forward to meeting my grandbaby. "Again boy, I can't help you if I don't know what's going on. So, if you won't talk to me at least go have a talk with God."

As good of a person my son is I know these past few months was hard on him. I know he wanted to be married before having a baby, but God had other plans. I truly believe God wanted to see how strong and committed my son really is. You see people can say they want to wait to have sex until their married. But when they break that promised they mad to God or themselves it's a choice. That's what God gave my son and Gabrielle, a choice to make.

"Mom, how did you dad do it? Not even God can change the past."

"Sounds like you need him, and if you talk to him he can lead you and Gabrielle in the right direction.

"Oh no, not after what I found out."

"Again Derrick, what was it because my guest are coming or Bible study."

"Call girl Mother Love. That's what Gabrielle, used to be. And the crazy part is I'm still in love with her."

"Ha… haa…haa, sounds like you need God, and

Jesus boy."

"What so funny? Who's to say that's my daughter?"

I started laughing again, if this isn't some craziness.
"My son's in love with a stripper and you have a
child with her. Boy don't you know everyone has a
past."

"Yeah you right but I' still getting a DNA test done.
I was a fool to actually believe Gabrielle."

"Boy what did Proverbs 3:5 say?"
"Trust in the Lord with all your heart and do not
lean on your own understanding." We both said.

"Now what's your point to that Mother Love?"

"Damn, son you've forgotten the things I've taught
you."

"What are you talking about Mom?"

"Now, haven't I taught you when there a problem
you can always go to God."

"Yeah but this is different."

"And how is that? Boy you know that girl loves you. That's the problem you'll so quick to run away when things get tough."

The doorbell rang and Derrick went to open it immediately.

"Carl what do you want?"

"Derrick, I'm glad I found you here, why don't you join us for Bible Study.

"Look Carl, I don't have time for your BS. I'm in the middle of a deep conversation with my mom about that manipulating chick Gabrielle."

"Boy, I'm not going to stand here and let you disrespect then woman you care about."

I looked at my son Derrick and the emotions he was trying to hide. This made me very concerned and I know God wants me to remind my son that him and Gabrielle made their baby out of love.

"Come on Derrick know you still love Gabrielle." Carl said.

"Look man, Love and attractions are two different things."

"So, what are you saying to me and Mother Love?"

"He'd better be saying how he's going to work things out with his family."

"Work things out ha! Not going to happen. Do you know the woman I cut ties with for Gabrielle?"

"Again son, that's because you love her."

"As I said I'm going to get a DNA test done."

"And where is that coming from? You know it don't even matter. Because if the results are positive then what?"

"Look man, I'll deal with that when I learn the truth."

The doorbell rang again and Derrick went to answer it.
"Oh, hell no!"

"What's up nephew."

It was my bother Leroy, and Keisha, I invited them to Bible study and somehow my brother actually showed up. I had to thank God for that because anyone that knew my brother, knew Armageddon might start inside the Church we went too at St. Anthony's. That's because of a lot of the women my brother messed with. But now it was time to have Church/Bible study in my house. God gave me a gift and that's to help these young folks see the light and that's what I intend to do.

19

Derrick

"I'm here sis, I told you I was coming. I'm serious about giving my life to God."

"Don't make me laugh Uncle Leroy. Giving your life to God is a serious commitment."

"And that's a commitment I'm honoring nephew."

"Derrick, I told you I'm having Bible study."

"I immediately turned my attention back to my Uncle. So, you feeling blessed now that you found you're daughter?"

"As a matter of fact, yes I am." Uncle Leroy said smiling.

"Mom, what's he really doing here?"

I was really hurting and upset. I didn't care about my Uncle's daughter coming into his life. I'm sure everyone heard about the nightmarish news I found out about Gabrielle. No one felt sorry for me and I wasn't looking for anyone to be sorry for me. But, my fiancée should have at least told me about her past and let me make the decision on staying or leaving. Because women asked for honesty in a man and I've been very open and honest about my pass Gabrielle, should have done the same. I put my head down and shook it. "Mom, how could you let these people in here at a time like this?"

"Look here boy everyone is welcomed in the hose of the lord." Mother Love said.

"You already know sis. Peter once said it wisely." Uncle Leroy said.

"That was Peter 4:9 right?" Carl said.

"Yes Carl, very good. Ladies They all say at the same time." Uncle Leroy said.

"Show hospitality to one another without grumbling." Both Mother Love and Keisha said.

As you can see Derrick, we all have Bible study here. Carl said smiling.

"Thanks Carl, and thanks you'll for coming. Now as I said before Derrick you need God and Jesus." Mother Love said smiling.

"Sis, aren't you going to welcome us?"

"Your already in the house Leroy. Now let's get started. And remember I'm not one of those women your use to dealing with."

"I never said you were. But I can be honest and say I never would have made this transition and got my daughter back in my life with God and you."

"Well, Leroy You are my brother. You may be my half- brother but still my brother."

"Hey Uncle Leroy, Where's Shemar?"

"The boy just got married let him and Natasha enjoy life."

"Whatever, who cares."

"You should care. Shemar is your cousin Derrick."

"Again mom, I'm happy for Shemar, but as of right now that's not important to me."

"Look Derrick, Gab is really hurting."

"What about me? You'll didn't think about that? But it's best I found out now instead of 5 or 10 years from now.

Now I was ready to lash out at anyone who had anything to say. It's as though they weren't see where I was coming from.

"Look boy, I Love you but you're acting like a complete jackass. Ladies tell him what I told you when things go bad.
Psalm 37:5."

Carl, Keisha, and Uncle Leroy were smiling and said.

"Commit your way to the lord trust in him and he will act."

Uncle Leroy started clapping.

"Very good people, I'm proud of you'll." Mother Love said.

"You see son how we give everything to God and that's what you should do. Let him do what he does and things will be alright." Mother Love said.

"Look, I don't need this Gospel stuff right now." I said storming out the house.

"Derrick wait man." Carl said.

"No Carl, let him be. All we can do is pray for him. Besides Pastor sharp will be here any moment.

Wrong sister Love Pastor Sharp is here. Now, it's time you young folks get some knowledge.

I walked passed Pastor Sharp, not even saying hi. I was really hurting and lost and right now I'm too angry to even think about God. Damn my poor little girl. All hell had broken loose since I found out about Gabrielle and her pass. This is just one big nightmare. What am I suppose to do now.

20
Gabrielle/Keisha

Gabrielle
2 days later.

All hell had broken loose that night at Half- Court bar. Ever since that bitch Keisha, had me talk about my pass to my now ex- Fiancée Derrick, me and my new baby have been lonely. My parents came to my house to watch her because they didn't want me alone with her. My Parents went on to tell me a lot of people who are new parents tend to do crazy things to a baby and not realize it until it's to late. I felt they were crazy to even think something like that about me, but I was still grateful to have my parents by my side. Especially after I told them what had happened. As a new mother it's my responsibility to protect my child and that's what I intend to do. I was on the phone with Mother Love whose Derrick's mom. I understand Mother Love, but wants done is done. Hold on somones ringing the doorbell.

As I open the door. "Well, now isn't this a

wonderful, oh no, Keisha what do you want?"
Keisha and I hadn't spoke to each other since that
night at Half-Court bar, and to be honest I was ok
with that because everything was going fine until
her ass had to get in my business. Also, I was upset
at the fact that she actually thought that I would join
her and Carl on their crazy ass fantasy. Keisha just
stared at me.
"Aren't you going to let me in?"

I just walked off but left the door opened.

"You ok Gab? Because I know I'm not, Carl, won't
talk to me or answer my text messages."

"That's your own fault." I said looking at her and
rolling my eyes.

"And how that?"

"You should've kept that ridiculous fantasy to
yourself. I mean what the hell were you thinking?"

"Now you know that's every man's fantasy Gab."

"But, you know Carl and Derrick are best friends
did you ever think of that?"

"Look I came to see if you were ok, not argue."
Keisha was right in a way. I mean what's done is

done and as I told Keisha, I'm a mother first before anything.

"No, I haven't been ok, I haven't been getting enough sleep. I just can't believe this is happening."

"Look Gab, every relationship gets hard at times. That's why I'm not worried about Carl."

"I understand that but it's a new year. I have a new born child I shouldn't be going through this."

"No, we shouldn't be going through this but this is the year we get it right."

"Your right girl, because God knows I've been through enough hard
times and tough times."

"I feel you."

I couldn't hold back my tears anymore. "My past is my past There was no one there paying for College, my books or tuition."

"Gab, I wish you would've come to me."

"And use that drug money you were making."

"Hey, you can't judge me there were no jobs hiring and beside it helped pay for my school tuition. I have my Associates. Plus, I help put money in your pocket by helping you stip."

"That's not the damn point Keisha too many of our people are getting caught up in this drug game.

Gab, look sometimes you got to do what got to do. And you stripping was one of those times."

"Again, Keisha that was the past Derrick did not need to know about that."

"Look, Gabrielle I need this bottle right now."

"Whatever, that's an excuse and you know it Keisha. Then you wonder why people look at us the way the do."

"And what's that supposed to mean. Look I don't this garbage in fact I need a drink. Some Heeney or E&J. will do nicely." Keisha said yelling at me.

"Keisha, since when are you drinking like this?"

"Come on Gab, Carl, won't talk to me these bottles gone take my mind off That you want some?"

"Look Keisha, I love you like a true sister, but you acting crazy right now."

"Why you say that?"

"I may want Derrick, and my family back but I'm a mother first. I will not be drinking around my daughter."

"Sometimes this is the answer." Keisha said holding her bottle up in the air.

"Keisha, have you lost your mind?"

"Look at least it's not drugs."

"But it's still an addiction and now you're an alcoholic really? Keisha, what's really going on here?"

"Ok Gab, it's not just Carl. This label company 9 Ounce records want to sign me. They love my voice and my talent. I feel I'm just not t=ready yet."

"Ok. Keisha but that bottle is not the answer. That's when you go to God and get the answer you looking for."

"I'm out of here." Keisha shouted out.

"Keisha, clam your voice down your niece is sleeping."

The doorbell rang again. "Now what? Who is it?"

Keisha went toward the door and as she opened it Uncle Leroy came in.

"Uncle Leroy!" I said with stunned eyes.
He looked at both of us.

"This is what you been doing? Carl's been asking for you."

"He walked out on me. Because of that bitch Rachel."

"Look you 2 want to go somewhere so you can work out you're problems."

"No, your sister's in a Demon in a bottle. She needs to get some help." Uncle Leroy said.

"I don't need help I need and want my manajatwa."

"This bitch hadn't learn yet."

"Look Keisha, it isn't happening at least not with me. Right now, I suggest we get you some help for this addiction of yours."

"I do not have an addiction."

Keisha stormed out the house.
"Keisha, you come back here."

"No, let her go. She has to figure this out on her own."

Uncle Leroy walked up to me hugging me. and just ran for Keisha. "Well be at Mother Love's house."

Keisha

I felt as though my heart was ready to burst out my chest. I never felt this way in my life. I've lost my man Carl, and my best friend, and the problems Carl and I have is just crazy. I was so upset and I evn wanted to surprise Carl for his birthday and have a threesome with Gabrielle. Now I know that might sound crazy but I remember how Gabrielle used to get down. I know all she really needed was a little something to drink and me to get her into getting our freak on. Plus, she still owed me a favor. I would have went to someone else but from what Rachel, put Carl and I though I was sure I could go to Gabrielle for the threesome I wanted to surprise Carl with. But, God wanted me to wake up from this crazy fantasy and that's ok with me. I'm kind of glad Gabrielle turned me down. Because the shit Carl and I are going through now because of Rachel should have woke me up but no it didn't. I was turned down and I might have lost my friendship with Gabrielle because of it. I went to the one person I knew wouldn't judge me and as I rang the doorbell I was let in right away.

"Hey Mother Love, we have to talk." I said smiling.

"What about you're drinking problem?"

I was totally caught off guard right away. I was embarrassed, despite the fact that I know Mother Love always means well. I looked at her sadly, taking in what she just asked me. I know she's disappointed in me. You see Mother Love is the closes person I have to a real mother. My real mom was never really there for me. I was raised by my Grandmother until she passed when I was in college.

"Well Keisha, are we going to talk about this drinking problem of yours or not?"

"I don't have a drinking problem. And how do you know about me
drinking anyway?"

"Girl, You, forgot word gets around. My other Nephew Shemar was headed in that same direction." Mother Love said

"Well I'm not Shemar. Now how you knew I been drinking."
"As my bothers employee,

"My former Employee." I said looking at Mother Love.

"Well ok, former employer it's my job to try and help people such as yourself."

"And I'm proud of you Leroy. God is proud of you." Mother Love said

"Uncle Leroy, I don't need help and my business shouldn't be out there."

"Carl, Mother love why don't we just start without her. It's obvious she doesn't want any help."

"Boy, you forgot Keisha comes here for Bible study. Now both you and Derrick have issues."

The doorbell rand and we all saw Derrick come inside. "Mother Love we have to talk."

"Well now, isn't God good?" Mother love said smiling.

"What's he doing here?" Derrick asked.

"Don't worry about it. Now I still owe you for that sucker punch." Carl said boiling up his fist.

"Not in my presents fellas." Uncle Leroy said. "Thanks Leroy, but don't worry I got this. Well continue the book of Proverbs later. Right now lets handle this. Keisha go on and have a set."

I did as I was told and walked by Derrick and Carl. The room was silent even Uncle Leroy was quiet.

I could tell I wasn't the only one Mother Love had something to say too. "People, I'm telling you now and I want you all to here this. Whatever, and I mean what ever your going through go to God. He has all the answers the day you stop having faith is the day you open your heart up for sin. And thats when the devil wants to knock down that wall God and his Angel have built for you."

"Amen sister." Carl said.

"Are you'll happy now? Look at the both of you. You'll both have fine Women. One of you with trust issues after his Fiancée gives birth."

"But Mother Love." Derrick said.

"Hush boy, I'm not finish now Carl, that fantasy of yours. It was just an idea of Keisha's and a birthday gift for you." Mother Love said.

"None of this is my fault." Carl said.
"Or mine mom. If she'd just told me about her being a stripper she would welcomed in our family."

"Boy, Gabrielle is welcomed in our family and I told you before
everyone has a past. Besides she was protected all the time

"And how's that?"

"Uncle Lero, was her pimp but he protected that girl all the time as well as Keisha.

"What?" Both Carl and Derrick shouted out.

"How am I suppose to handle that? Mother Love."
Derrick asked.

"Look boy, I keep telling you everyone has a past."

"Mother Love I have to agree with Derrick. How
are we suppose to handle this?" Carl said.

She seems to have all the answers and knows
everything.

MOTHER LOVE looked at all of us.
"Look at the all of you. You're all acting like
Demons in a battle waiting to come out."

"Oh really?"
"Yes really. You'll are letting the devil win."

"You tell them Mother Love." I said.

"Now Keisha, now after I say what I have to say we
going to listen to some Gospel music in here."

The thought entered my mind on what Mother Love
had to say. Because I don't think I ever saw her this
disappointed in any of us ever. I decided too listen
to here what Mother Love was saying.

"Keisha, I don't know what made you think you can go to your best friend and ask her to do something crazy like that. Girl you know Carl and Derrick are best friend. Did you ever think what that would do to their friendship? I sure you didn't think that through. That's why reading and understanding the book of Proverbs is important."

I was quiet and listening to Mother Love.
"But Mother Love." Derrick said.

"Hush boy, because if you really understood the book of Proverbs, you wouldn't have interrupted me. You'd have the wisdom to listen. Now both You and Carl need to Thank God for the women in your life."

The doorbell rang and as Mother Love went to answers it Uncle Leroy came inside. Derrick immediately went to swing on his Uncle but Carl stopped him right away.
"Uncle Leroy you've got some nerve pimping my woman."

"Ha…ha…ha…ha…, Boy that's what I do. Besides it was before you 2 started dating."

"Also, your Uncle Leroy, stopped doing that long time ago. Especially since God has brought him and his daughter to each other isn't that right Leroy."

Uncle Leroy hesitated scratching his head. "Well."

"Leroy! This is why some of our brother don't show respect to our sisters now."

Uncle Leroy kept laughing.
"Don't worry sis. They can come see me anytime."

I watched Carl shake his head usually he'd laugh along Uncle Leroy but this is a situation that he wasn't laughing at all.

"Look Mother Love, we just want our women back. Keisha let's forgive each other and get pasted this.

Uncle Leroy walked up to me. "I understand son God understands what you'll want out of your women.. But first let me explain something to you'll."

"And what's that?" Derrick asked.

Uncle Leroy looked at both Carl and Derrick.

"Understand this fellas, a man can be successful but for that success to continue it takes a strong woman to be in his life."

"All this positive energy in here. This is why people love coming to Mother Loves house. Derrick can you give my sister Gabrielle another chance she's a good woman bro."

"I never said she wasn't I just don't know if I can trust her."

MOTHER LOVE grabbed Derrick by the arm "Boy haven't I taught you anything? Talk to God, he's always listening. He hears and delivers."

"Amen." Uncle Leroy said.

"Come on with this. Bible talk Mom."

"Derrick, free your mind Gabrielle loves you. Everyone comes with baggage when starting a relationship."

"And all you need to do is help Gabrielle unpack that baggage." Carl said.

"I can do that." Uncle Leroy said.

"That's my lady you talking about Uncle Leroy."

"That's ok, she's still a woman. One that I respect dearly." Uncle Leroy said smiling.

"Yo man!" Derrick shouted.

"Relax boy, and go get you're woman. Use all that energy you have into getting her back."

I looked at Carl and Derrick give each other a five and shack each others hand.

"You know Carl, their right."

"Yeah they are. Keisha can you forgive me?"

"I'm sorry for punching you Carl.

"It's behind us brother."

I watched both Carl and Derrick hug one another.

"Thank you God, I love to seeing Black Men work through their problems without Guns and Violence." Mother Love said.

"You're right Mother Love there's enough killing in the US as it is." Derrick said.

"We need to embrace each other. And remember we all have black power in us." Carl said.

"You got that right, now go get your women They may have some friends I haven't met yet." Uncle Leroy said.

"I'm with you bro. But I made an appoint first thing in the mourning. Mom thanks again." Derrick said.

I watched both Carl and Derrick shake hands as their friendship bonded even more. "You know Derrick we both have a reputation to uphold. We were once known for getting some of the finest women out here in NYC. Now God called us to go get our ladies."

"Wait Carl, I never said I was getting back with Gabrielle, especially after the stunt she pulled I'm still not sure if I can trust her."

I swallowed hard, because after all this, Satan is still trying to keep Derrick and Gabrielle apart. I'm praying God puts a shield up for us all.

Uncle Leroy

21

Next day.

I wasn't used to listening to what my sister had to say, when it came to my business. I felt no one but God, understood the pain I was in since loosening my beloved Michelle. But, since my daughters come into my life, slowly I'm becoming a better and new man. It's been the better part of a year now, since my nephew Shemar got married and God had my daughter come into my life. She was almost one of my employees. Now, I'm looking to change the way I do things and that's what I wanted my nephew Derrick to understand. Because he's a new father and I really don't want him being out of his daughter's life like I was out of mine. Although I never even knew I had a daughter until the night she was about to be my employee. I can count on one hand how many times my sister, Mother Love said "God, love the progress your making Leroy." I had just left my sisters place. We were supposed to have Bible study there, but instead my nephew and his best friend Carl, my young protégé had women problems. Not to mention they had just had something big they had to settle between themselves. My nephew Derrick, found out his daughter's mother, who is his fiancée in my opinion found out that she use to work for me. I did my best protecting her from what was another part of the job and the extra things that came along with it. Right now I had one of the church quire women in my home. Her name was Chenille, Chenille, was a fine chocolate sexy woman the only problem was she was a married woman. Now in the past this would not be a problem at all for me, but I'm changing my ways and this is something Chenille wasn't understanding. "So, are we going to start this dance Leroy? I'm ready to feel you babe." Chenille said whispering seductively.

She looked up and down my body as she poured E&J in our cups. What Chenille didn't know is I was changing my ways and drinking was one of them. As Chenille went on to drink her cup of E&J she walked up to me and I knew the next move was mine. Her eyes was meeting mine as she put her drink down as she came ready for our lips to meet I smiled with a devilish grin saying… "Let's read Proverbs 7: 1-5." I said pulling out my Bible on my phone.

1. My son, keep my commands within you. 2. Keep my commands and you will live; Guard my teachings as the apple of your eyes. 3. Bind them on the tablet of your heart. 4. Say to wisdom, "You are my sister," and insight, you are my relative." 5. They will keep you from the adulterous woman, from the wayward woman with her seductive words."

"Wait, so what are you trying to say Leroy?"
"I'm saying temptation can be a very hard thing to overcome. That's the reason you can't give in to

temptation, you can't let the devil win Chenille. I said glancing at her up and down."

'Now Solomon, didn't say we as men couldn't look.' But I wasn't even going to lust for Chenille. Instead I'm going to ask her the same thing a woman would ask her husband.

"Chenille where's your husband?"

She immediately gave me an annoyed look. "Look I'm just asking because I'm not with that adultery, it's a game we use to play. In the past Chenille and I would have already been in my bedroom getting busy, while at my sister's house she told me we needed to talk and I agreed and invited her to my place. "You came here to talk, so let's talk." "I'm pregnant Leroy." "Say what?"

"You heard me I'm pregnant."

"Let me guess, you don't know who the father is now?"

"Oh, I know who the father is Leroy and it isn't you."

"Well that fine because I don't want anymore kids anyway. So, what's the problem, and congratulations by the way."

"The problem is my husband doesn't want anymore kids."

"I don't blame him I mean we're damn near 60 years old."

"Also, he won't have sex with me and I'm horny as hell my hormones is spinning out of control. You men think the shit women go through is just a game. Your completely wrong."

I know Chenille really wants me to be her man after all these years 7 to be exact. She always said she would be complete if I was the man in her life. We met at her daughter's college graduation. Her daughter Nikki was of course one of my employees she moved to Manhattan. Nikki wanted to be a Lawyer, so she decided to go to John jay. I was very happy for Nikki, but through College Nikki, Gabrielle, Keisha was my girls I can count on to help me recruit young women for my business. I watched over them making sure some desperate man didn't step over board. This women, was determined to succeed in life, and I was the one to make sure they did. When Chenille found out I was the one who helped her daughter the college because she couldn't afford it she thanked me that same night. I didn't find out she was married until months later but at least 2 times a year we'd meet up and being that it's a new year I wanted her and a lot of other people to know slowly I'm being coming a changed man.

"Leroy, stop playing you know you want this. And you know pregnant pussy is the best." That's young pregnant pussy. Woman you old."

The hell with you Leroy. Everyone knows you not shit. I'm out of here." "God bless you Chenille."

"I'm glad Chenille is going to represent your friends."

"So am I, and congratulations again."

I'm not at all a perfect man, but none of us are but one things for sure I was going to meet my sister at church and turn it up in the mourning.

Mother Love
22

I was on the phone with my son, most of the mourning as I was getting ready for Church. My son Derrick, still was not ready to forgive his Fiancée, and I told him to be there for her because she just had his baby. All he kept saying was he's going to be there for his child. I prayed to God that my son can find it in his heart to forgive Gabrielle, because he needs to realizes the maturity of being a husband. As I stepped out the house and locked my door.

"Mother Love, Mother Love."

I turned around and looked to see who was calling me, when I saw who it was I couldn't believe it. It was my neighbor Marlene, and her abusive husband James. Just last month I had a serious talk with the both of them. I invited them to my house and explained to them that their daughter will remember what she sees from the both of you. I understood how much they wanted their marriage to work especially being newly weds. I suggested that they go to counselling and told them they have nothing to be embarrassed about.

I tried to tell Derrick, the same thing but as much as I love my son the boy can be stubborn as hell. "Mother love, we did what you suggested. Now we can talk with one another without getting into arguments." James said.

"Most importantly, I'm not on public assistance anymore. I'm in school now and I'm working at BlackLoveEntertainment." Marlene said.

"That's good news, but What is BlackLoveEntertainment?" I asked.

"It's a magazine company and the company is helping pay for my college. We wanted to thank you for your prayers Mother Love." Marlene said.

"Yes, our marriage is at a good place now thanks to you." James said.

"Thank you, both of you but it's all Gods doing and the fact that you both never lost your faith in him, and you'll actually went to him for help." I said.

"Your right Mother Love, but it was your prayers and wisdom and knowledge that helped us in the first place." James said.

I was used to hearing things like this from people. James was on his way to what I call the dark side and that's because he didn't get into none and I mean none of the city jobs he took test for and after going through the process of everything he applied for. I mean he did everything but make the academy at NYPD, Correction, School Safety, and NYPD Traffic. I could tell he was hurt and disappointed but God has something else in store for him that's what I told James. So, instead of taking it out on his wife he needs to cherish her and be happy to have her in his life. James was in complete silence, just like he is now. "I'm proud of the both of you why don't you'll come to Church with me and praise God."

"That's exactly what we're going to do Mother Love, because we have some celebrating to do." Marlene said.

"What's the celebration?" I asked being curious.

"We're pregnant." They both said.

"Congratulations to you both. You'll must let me throw your baby shower."

"I'd love that Mother Love thank you." Marlene said.

Instead of me driving to Church and wasting gas they offered me a ride instead. While inside their Audi car I was listening to what these two lovers had to say to me. "Mother Love we're both excited on having our first child together, but there is one problem." James said. "And what's that?" I asked.

"Marlene's mom doesn't think I'm good enough for her daughter. She thinks I'm going to use her kindness which I find crazy. Just last week when I met her and we were having dinner the woman asked me if I know how to pray. I was really offended."

"James I told you not to pay her any attention." Marlene said.

"Now hold on you two. James you have to understand the woman is just protecting her baby."

"Wait a minute Mother Love I'm a grown woman."

"Marlene, I get that but you going to always be your mothers baby. My son Derrick is grown and he's still my baby. So understand James you've got to let God work on her mother and you continue to show Marlene the respect she deserves. You both have a child coming into this world so you'll don't have time for who approves of your relationship. As long as God is in your lives you both have nothing to worry about."

"Your right Mother Love, they can take their problems to God." Marlene said.

15 minutes later inside St. Anthony's.
"So, Mother Love, I have to say you've done a lot to motivate people in our community, and our Church. You've touched people's hearts and I'd like for your voice to be heard today. Pastor Sharp said to me.

Pastor Sharp had become a good friend of mine and he's now on his 3rd marriage and I must say God's blessed him a lot. Because being a single father all these years 18 to be exact. He lost his first wife to cancer and his second wife Desire who happened to be a good friend of mine lost her life when she gave birth to their daughter. Once word got out that Pastor Sharp's second wife Nicole passed a lot of these church heifers didn't hesitate at all in throwing themselves at the Pastor every chance they got. No matter how good of a man of God Pastor Sharp was these women knew he was still a man. A man with needs and I've seen these church women too many times in action. Now when his present wife Joan came into his life he was full of joy and laughter and the reason I know this is because he'd always tell me and he even brought her over my house a few times. I welcomed Joan with open arms and now that it was time to speak in front of all these people I was not at all about to let God, myself and the Paster down.

I stood in front of the people at St Anthony's and while all eyes were on me I picked my head up and as started looking at the crowd I was smiling across the room. "Good mourning everyone, I'm glad the Lord has brought all of you here. I'm not surprised that Pastor has asked me to come here and speak with you'll I want to remind you'll about keeping your faith and trusting God. You see Job was tested about his faith to God. He felt everything was taken from him. Other people felt his blessing were just given to him. But when he started to lose his faith and accused God of injustice."

Wait, that's not true. Job suddenly gave up because things were taken from him." A man in the audience said.

You always have at least one person who doesn't believe. It's always that one person. "Bother please be silent." Pastor sharp said.

No, it's ok Pastor. Brother read the book of Job again, that goes for all of you to. You'll see what I was about to say before I was interrupted. In Job 28:28. He say's the fear of the Lord is wisdom and to depart from evil is understanding. Because Satan always tries to come into your life everyone because we all are trying to get a better relationship with God everyday." I said looking at that brother and then the audience.

Only time will tell if my message got through some if not all the people who attended here today at St. Anthony's. I'm hoping my son is in here somewhere and I'm hoping my words have touched someone's heart. Because having faith and keeping hope alive is a powerful thing.

Carl

23

After hearing what Mother Love had to say, everyone that was at St. Anthony's was clapping including Pastor Sharp. My mind was consumed for these past few days, including today here at St. Anthony's. I was hoping that giving my time to God would make me feel better. I still was upset what's been happening in my life lately. I'm talking from the situation Keisha, and I got ourselves into dealing with Rachel, going back and forth to court has really taking a toll on us both. It's very emotional. I found out Keisha wanted to surprise me for my bday but have a threesome, what's crazy is that it was with my boy's Fiancée Gabrielle, I mean they just had a baby together. I don't know what Keisha, was thinking as if she didn't learn her lesson from the situation with Rachel, what's crazy is that it was with my God daughter's mom and then witnessing the breakup of my boy Derrick and Gabrielle, trying to claim Derrick down I got sucker punched. All I did was try and claim Derrick down and I got sucker punched, usually I'd be ready to go at someone who put there hands on me, but I'm slowly becoming a changed man, and it's not a bad thing. Just being around people like

Mother Love has been a blessing. I broke things off with Keisha, all these things we've been going through is just crazy and it's been too much. As much as I still love Keisha, I just needed a time out. When the mourning services was over I stepped outside for some air. I shook my head saying to myself what the hell was Keisha thinking? Because now her and Gabrielle's friendship is ruined.

"Leaving so soon?"

I turned around to see this beautiful brown skinned woman look at me. She was sexy, she had on a black dress and stood about 5,3.
"Well aren't you going to say anything?" She said smiling.
I smiled and looked at her. "I'm sorry, my names Carl and what's your name?"

"Mary and I must say Carl, your leaving Church kind of early."

"Who said I was leaving?"

"I did, let's go somewhere and talk now."

"Keisha, what are you doing here?"

"The same reason you're here Carl, now let's go."
"Halleujah! Wasn't that mourning service wonderful?" Uncle Leroy asked.

"What happened? Why are you'll out here?" Mother Love asked.

For some air, by the way Mother Love that was a wonderful thing you said to the Church today." I said.

"Yes, there's nothing like a good word for people to hear especially when it's coming form the heart. Mother Love great job Carl it was nice meeting you." Mary said as she went back inside the Church.

"Look if you'll excuse me I'm leaving early." I said as I walked off.

"Carl! Carl! What's really going on? Why you leaving Church? It's not like you."

Keisha was right it wasn't like me at all but the things we been through these past few weeks and all this drama is just too much.

"Why are you angry at me?" Keisha asked.

Keisha was right, I was angry, angry at myself and the fact that I told God I was going to change my ways. It just wasn't happening as quickly and easily as I thought. I can remember when Derrick would always talk about how he was a reflection of his mother. Mother Love is such a respected woman not just in the Church but in the community. I would tell him he's his own man and although Mother Love is his mother he doesn't have to be involved in the Church like she is. "I once told Derrick he has his own dreams and desires and

whoever don't like it that's on them."

"You said that to him? Now you know Mother Love wants him to become a Pastor. And I believe God works on everyone, but he wants them to work on themselves. Just look at Uncle Leroy, since finding out he's got a daughter he's become a changed man."

"You actually believe that?"

"Yes, he has changed in his own way. Look let's go some where besides your place."

We drove off in Keisha's Infiniti and as I drove off in her car only God knew where Keisha wanted me to drive us. I just listened to where she wanted me to take her. "Keisha, a lot of people might think I'm a bad influence on you. Also, they may think I'm no good for you." I said stopping at a red light.

Carl, didn't you just tell me what you told Derrick about not caring what people think?"

"Yeah, I did."
"Then take your own advice. That's the problem with some people they don't practice what they preach."
"Look Keisha, where ever it is you want me to drive to we're going to have a serious talk." I stepped on the gas once we were on Eastern parkway just to let Keisha know I was serious.

Keisha

24

For almost 2 hours Carl and I was talking with one another at Atlantic Motor. I'd asked God for some time now to help Carl and I get out that situation we were in with Rachel. Also, our relationship had become a bit complicated and that was something I just didn't need in my life. I explained to Carl how I would be taking my music more serious. I let him know how grateful I was and in these troubled times we were going through. "Carl, every relationship has it's ups and downs. There's couples who go through far worst than what we go through."

"First of all I told you I was tired of the drama. I know that sounds crazy coming from me but it's the truth. I'm giving my life over to God."

"Carl, I know you, you can't just turn your life around over to God just like that. And you keep talking about drama, that situation with Rachel was to spice things up in our bedroom." I said looking at Carl as I took my shoes off.

"Spice things up in the bedroom? I'm out of here."

"Carl wait."
"Carl turned around and looked at me. Okay, you want me to stay? Just answer me this one question why didn't you tell me Gabrielle was the woman you wanted to surprise me with on my birthday?"

"I wanted to surprise you Carl, and after everything we been going through I wanted to make your birthday special." I said lowering my head.

"Look Keisha, you're not a lesbian."

"No, but you know I love my pussy eaten every once in a while. What woman doesn't? Look Carl, I asked you to come here to let you know I was taking my music serious. Also, so we can start fresh. I don't need know man judging me."

"Woman, all I'm saying is…"

Suddenly, my lips was on Carl's and he welcomed me with no problem. "Why you look so surprised." I said while my breast was rubbing against his chest.

I wanted Carl, I wanted him to touch me, kiss me and for us to get busy. I was horny, and I was not about to be turned down by Carl.
Carl, I whispered. "Why don't you take your clothes off?"
I said headed to the bathroom.

"You sure?" Carl asked.

I nodded and within a minute Carl and I found our way into th shower together. The next thing I know Carl was on his knees with his tongue between my legs. I was holding his head moaning loudly. 30

minutes later Carl and I was making love on the bed. "Wait where's the condom?"

"Don't you worry my pull out game is on point."

"Oh, Carl." I said out loud.

I clanged to his back as I climaxed. Carl kept kissing my neck, then I wrapped my arms around his waist and closed my eyes. My entire body was hot our lips was connected. Carl became aggressive and I loved it. He started sucking my breast and damn it it felt so good. Carl put his tongue back into my mouth and as his hands slid down my backside and he started palming my ass. We made love and I mean it was passionate love so much that we climaxed together. I let out a loud scream because of how god it felt. "I love you Carl always remember that."

"I love you too Keisha." Carl said.

"Carl, we learned a big lesson that day and I know your bday is coming, but let's not ever let a situation like Rachel's come between us."

"In Jesus name". Carl said.

We both kissed each other and said Amen. Our love making continued and lasted for about 3 hours I never came so much. When Carl got up to go to the bathroom he feel to the floor and although I wanted to laugh I asked was he alright. He told me he caught a Charlie horse. "Ha…ha…ha." I laughed even harder than before.

"What's so funny?" Carl asked.

"Oh, it's nothing I'm just happy with myself."

"What you mean."

"I mean I did my job as a woman."

We both learned a valuable lesson and because of the situation with Rachel. Plus Gabrielle and I are not on good terms because off me wanting to please Carl for his birthday. When it was time for Carl and myself to check out the hotel both of us was feeling good. "Omg, Carl look at this." I said.
We both couldn't believe our eyes. Both Carl and I were stunned. "Mary, what are you doing with her?"
"Hello, to you too Carl."
This day just had to be ruined. I 'd say the devil's behind this because Carl and I left the room without even praying. You see ever time the devil sees people that trying to get close to God he interferes. "Mary, my man Carl asked you a question. What are you doing with Rachel?"

"Excuse me I don't owe you any explanation."

"You right Mary, but I'm telling you tis woman is bad news. You have to believe me on this."

We both watch Mary and Rachel kiss each other and walked off.
"Carl, let's just go."

"No, Keisha God would want us to help her. We got to help Mary before she ends up in a bad situation."

"Look Carl, as much as I love you. You can be blind by some of these Jezebels out here. Mary is Pastor Sharp's daughter that's why I pulled you away from her. Believe me I know you wanted to hit that." I said to Carl.

"Ha…ha… You right."

"Look Carl God gives us choices to make and that's their choice."

"Wooo… weee…Listen to you I'm proud to hear you speak about a God babe." Carl said kissing me.

I'd never let him know it made me a little jealous. But the point is our relationship or whatever this is is back on track.

Derrick

25

Dr. Wave sat at his desk tentatively, listening to me speak my heart out. I kept talking about my problems about trusting Gabrielle, and the fact that we just had a baby. "Dr. Wave I mean how am I supposed to put my trust in her after finding out she use to work for my Uncle?"

"Well what do you find wrong with that?"

'The fact that the Doctor asked me that question just told me I might as well come out and tell him.' "You see Dr. Wave my Uncle Leroy is a former pimp and I mean he's a true pimp."

"What do you mean former Pimp?"

"Well, he's now changed his life. All because he's daughter is back in his life. He's more about having God in his life."

"Well, there's nothing wrong with that. Is there?"
"No, Doc there isn't but let me just stick to the

subject because Gabrielle and I were ready to be married."

Dr. Wave, didn't show any kind of emotions. He's a true professional and I respect that. He sat there and kept listening. He watched me boil my fists because I was still so mad at Uncle Leroy, Gabrielle and most of all my mom. "Yes, Doc, my mom Mother Love told me Gabrielle worked for Uncle Leory way before Gabrielle and I started seeing each other. I just feel like one of them should have told me and that person is Gabrielle."

"Well, Derrick since you let me know how much you and your family have a close relationship with God. Also, you explained to me how much Mother Love wants people having a relationship with God."

"Yes, yes I did say that, but I tell you Doc, I'm just not sure I can do it. I know I told Mother Love and Carl I'd work it out with Gabrielle."

"Well Derrick, remember this relationship never really died."

"What do you mean?"

"Think about it. It's usually because of people's ego's attitude and their ignorance that kills a relationship.

"So, you're saying me and Gabrielle are not through."

"Not at all. Derrick a true relationship is when 2 people can tell each other any and everything."

"With no secrets and lies of course."

"No secrets and lies. Derrick never forget who helped and stayed with you through difficult times."

I had to be true to myself, Gabrielle was the one praying for me when thing we're not going my way at times.

"You're right I'm going to talk to Gabrielle and tell her let's make it work." I said.

I was starting to feel better and I watched Dr. Wave smile. But deep down I knew things are not going to be so easy as it sounds.

"Derrick relationship only last long when couples choose to keep it. Fight for and make it work. Remember to Laugh, live and love each other."

I put my jacket on and shook Dr. Waves hand. As I stated he's a true professional. I was going to take his advice and tell Gabrielle how important trust is to me and how we can make this work. Something inside me just knew Gabrielle was going to be happy to see me. I also can't wait to see my baby girl. Maybe coming here talking about my situation wasn't such a bad thing at all.

Gabrielle
26

This situation with Derrick and my past coming to hunt me is just plan crazy. This is all the devil's doing, but I must say Derrick still mad his own choice. I got a call from Mother Love to come to her house. I worked my ass off through college and did what I had to help me get through. I mean I wasn't the first nor would I be the last to be a striping by night and working toward my goal by day. Yes, I'm kind of ashamed at me doing the stripping thing but it's in the past. The only thing is I kept that part of my life from Derrick. As I approached Mother Loves house I could hear people talking. I rang the doorbell and as Carl opened the door.

"Mother Love I want to thank you for everything. Well look who's here." Carl said as he walked back toward Keisha.

"Yes, Mother Love We've learned to just have patience.

"Let the others get here Now Car, have you taken care of that alcohol problem?"

"Yes, before it really became a real problem I've gotten help. Keisha even came to support me."

I finally walked inside. "What are you doing here?" I asked looking at Mother Love and then Keisha.

"I was invited Look Gab, again I'm sorry I just wanted you to be honest with your man."

"Again, Keisha that's none of your business that was for me to tell Derrick." I said as I was right in Keisha's face ready to slap fire out of her.

"Look ladies, I asked you both to come here and heal and forgive and where's the baby?" Mother Love asked.

"With my parents, and Mother Love I have forgiven her but as you'll can see she hasn't changed so I'm just wasting my time.

"I have changed. I'm a woman of God and trust me someday all of this will make sense."

"You're the reason Derrick Walked out on me and my Daughter. But he felt stupid when he got those DNA results in the mail."

"Look ladies, everything happens for a reason. Gab
That was Derrick's choice to walk out." Mother
Love said.

"But Mother Love." I was really becoming confused
here.

"But nothing if a man can't see what your worth
then move on." Keisha said as she looked at Carl.

"Oh, let me guess this is when you ladies team up
and talk about
Sister Hood?" Carl asked.

"Look ladies, you too Carl I want you'll to grab
hands and realize we are children of God and we're
not going to apologize for it." Mother Love said.

"Your right Mother Love, Brother John once said.
No one saw God, but if we love one another God
abides in us, because his love is perfected in us.
Now give me some love Uncle Leroy you too
Mother Love."

Carl immediately tried to give Mother Love a high
five.

"Sit down boy you don't get a trophy or spreading the word of god."

The doorbell rang. I went over to Keisha hugging her and started smiling.

Derrick walked inside. This time Mother Love went to answer the door. Well I was not about to be fooled by Derrick good looks, and I was still curious as to why Mother Love invited me here. People like Derrick got my good looks confused. I should go back to being that bitch that a lot of Negros out here wanted. Just for a 30 minute lap dance I'd make $500 easy. But those were my hustling days, now I'm a Mother and a single one at that never in my life did I expect this at all. I thought Derrick and I were a good match and we'd never run into problems but it is what it is and now it's about facing reality.

"Derrick, don't just stand there. Come inside Derrick."

"Mother Love what are you trying to do?" I asked looking at Derrick.

"Hi everyone." Derrick said.

"Mother Love why are you'll doing this?"

I was really curious as to why she invited me and everyone here. She asked me to come to Church with her and Her son Derrick I can understand but I have to realize where Mother is coming from and who she is a women with a great heart.

"Look, I told you'll need healing and this is the place to do it."

"Having Church in the house Mother Love?" Carl asked.

"Why not God is everywhere." Uncle Leroy said.

"And there's nothing wrong with that. Now get ready for bible study. Mother Love said pulling out her bible.

"Wait, there's something I have to say." Derrick said looking at everyone.

"Can't it wait?" Keisha said.

"She's right son whatever it is I'm sure it can wait?"

I could see everyone was excited about being here after all and that this was something Mother Love probably prayed on. I can see God answered her prayers.

"Look, Uncle Leroy sir, this can't. Carl again I'm sorry for punching you."
"It's in that past man all is forgive. But not forgotten, right now let's focus on pleasing God.

"Gabrielle, I'm sorry for not believing you. I had to be sure that's my little girl you had.

"Good for you boy." Uncle Leroy said smiling.

"Well now you know. She is you're baby."

Derrick came and grabbed my hand. "Your right, and that's why in front of everyone here. I'm letting you know I'm ready to come home. Babe I want you to be my wife Gabrielle Davis will you marry me.

"Marry you?" I looked at Derrick smiling.

"Yes, marry me let's have a wedding."

"Derrick, I want a real marriage not just a wedding. I didn't just want a baby with you I wanted a family."

"We can have that babe."

"No, we can't Derrick. It's not just about my past you didn't respect."

"I understand Gab, you did what you had to do to survive."

Keisha immediately jumped in Derrick's face. "Yes, she did, but you just don't get it Derrick."

"Keisha, stay out of this."

"Yeah, don't you have a man of your own?"

"Yes she has a man." Carl said looking Derrick in the eye.

"Let everyone say Amen." Uncle Leroy shouted out.

Everyone shouted Amen and with smiles on their faces. It's amazing how Mother Love can bring peace to peoples live.

"Carl, you didn't? You and Keisha?"

"Yes, they did. You see they both believe in God and the Kingdom of Heaven." Uncle Leroy said.

"I see where you're going with this." Uncle Leroy.

"Me too. I'm proud of the both of you for getting baptized." Mother Love said.

"Then everyone Matthew 6:33." Uncle Leroy.

Everyone including myself except Derrick said. "Seek first the Kingdom of God and his righteousness, and all these things will be added to you."

The doorbell rang again and this time we saw Pastor Sharp come inside. Keisha and Carl were smiling.

"Thank you, Uncle Leroy and Pastor Sharp and of course you too Mother Love.

I was happy for Carl and Keisha.

"Congrats girl, now Derrick I want a man that's going to trust me. A man that loves me wouldn't do anything to lose me."

"So, what you saying? You don't want us being together?" Derrick said.

"Derrick, you made your choice when you walked out on me and your daughter. Because of my past."

"Yeah, but if you would've just told me." Derrick shouted out.

Whammm!

"Boy stop raising your voice." Mother Love said as she slapped Derrick.

"Look Derrick, I'm living on my terms and if I'm going to be involved with someone they've got to accept my past and respect me as a woman."

"Look Gabrielle."

"Look man, you need to chill." Carl said.

Derrick turned around and boiled his fists as if he was ready to swing on Carl. "What?" Derrick shouted out.

"You won't sucker punch me this time." Carl said.

"No he won't. Now Carl you should know better quickly Proverbs 3:31. Carl!" Uncle Leroy said out.

"Yes sir. Do not envy a man violence, and do not choose any of his way's." Carl said.

"So in other words do not feed into that fighting your brother." Uncle Leroy said.

"I'm out of here I don't need to hear this." Derrick said storming out the house.

"Derrick." Carl said trying to stop Derrick from leaving.

"No Carl, let him leave. He needs help and only God can do that now all we can do is pray." Mother Love said.
I walked up to Mother Love hugging her and Keisha hoping that all of this will one day work itself out.

Mother Love

27

I nodded my head as we all just watched my son Derrick storm out my home. It amazes me how these young people are so quick to give up on a relationship, especially after just having a baby. I was trying to bring Derrick and Gabrielle back into one another's arms, but my son just let the devil in his head instead of listening to God. He completely just walked off, just like that and without eve saying goodbye.

"Let's go everyone it's time to get into these scripts." I said as everyone sat down.

As every looked at Pastor Sharp smiling at us we all was happy to just be here in my home. Carl was excited about hearing the good word. Pastor Sharp stood about 6,2 and was brown skin, you'd never see him without a suit. Pastor Sharp was a respected man in the community, even when his wife 2 years ago passed away he never stopped preaching the word of God.

"Mother Love, I want you to do the teaching today. I just love the way you touch these young people hearts. It appears well just have to start without my daughter." Pastor Sharp said.

He didn't have to ask twice I looked at everyone and smiled. "Are you'll ready to learn today? "Yes we are Mother Love." Keisha said smiling.

"I want to say there's rules to praying. Just like there's rules to the game of dating, there rules to following the word of God and his ten commandments. There different kinds of praying just like there are different kind of rules to different job, different sports. There's different kind of rules to praying."

"Amen sister. That's my sister speaking." Leroy said.

"Thank you Leroy. Now everyone remember what the book of John said about praying, let's read John 15:7."

Everyone opened their bibles and read out. "If you abide in me, and my words abide in you, ask whatever you wish, and it will be done for you." Everyone said.

These past few weeks have been hard on everyone in this room including myself. I knew how badly Derrick wanted a family of his own. I ask God to forgive me in the part I played by not telling him, but I wanted Gabrielle to do that on her own. These people needed healing and reminding none of us are perfect. We must have the ability to forgive one another and these are times God wants to see how much can we really forgive the person who hurt us. The doorbell rang again and Carl went to answer it. "Oh my God, Chenille what are you doing here?" Leroy said.

I invited my brothers play thing over because when I ran into her at St. Anthony's Church she told me and she said it's a possibility that it's my brothers baby. Chenille was like a widow I don't know why my brother would get himself caught up with a married woman. But I was going to find out, because I could have a new niece or nephew.

"Pastor Sharp why don't you continue bible study for us my sister and I have to talk to this old woman." Leroy said as he grabbed my arm pulling me to the side. "This is not my baby. She's a married woman for God sake."

"Then why would you put yourself in this position in the first place?" I said looking at Leroy.

"It isn't his baby." Chenille said.

"But how do you know that?" I asked.

"Look the two of you especially you Leroy, these kids I'm having."

"Wait, wait, you said kids. Woman you can't carry twin at your age." Leroy shouted out.

"That's way you'll need to talk. I mean come on Leroy in Jesus name."

The doorbell rang again and the last person I was expecting was Pastor Sharp's daughter. We never meet in person so everyone including myself wanted to make her feel welcomed. "Oh, hell no!" Carl shouted out.

"This bitch is Pastor Sharps daughter?"

I couldn't believe it myself Rachel is Pastor Sharp's daughter. Rachel, just walked passed everyone giving her father Pastor Sharp a hug.

"Carl, Keisha, Chenille outside now!"

My brother Leroy shouted out loud enough for everyone in the house to hear him. I guess he really wanted his presence to be felt by Chenille.

Uncle Leroy

28

The fifth teen minute ride felt more than fifth teen minutes. Both Carl and Keisha came along with me. Pastor Sharp stayed with Mother Love he gave me the keys to St. Anthony's, my sister can sometimes be a bit too caring. Mother Love is a woman of God so I couldn't be to hard on her, but getting in my business and the way I do business has gotten out of hand. Chenille being pregnant has nothing to do with me, she should be celebrating with her husband but the man is never there to take care of his lady. I glanced at Carl and Keisha, I knew they are very happy after what they've over come. Now was not good time for happiness, because I don't think Carl or Keisha was expecting the guess that showed up. In fact I know they weren't no one would have ever thought Rachel was Pastor Sharp's daughter. I'm glad I brought them out of my sister's house right away. I drove us in front of St. Anthony's, I wanted everyone including myself to claim down. I tried my best to keep my cool myself I wanted to set an example to Carl who is like a son to me just like Derrick is. This is the type of situation I warned Carl and Derrick about and that's because I didn't want them running into women like Chenille. "Leroy, we can have something special."

"Woman for the last time you're a married woman, and your pregnant with your husband's baby."

"Congratulations, how far along are you?" Keisha asked.

"Thank you, I'm about 3 months."

"Uncle Leroy, how and why would you get caught up in this situation?" Carl said.

Look Carl, this situation isn't even complicated. Chenille's going to her husband and let him know her situation. That's for them to decided if their going to have this baby. It's not my problem."

"Hold up, that's the reason Mother Love said how do you know it's her husbands. Uncle Leroy you've been sleeping with this woman?" Carl said.

I wondered if Carl was defending this woman because Keisha was there or because his love life is back on track. I parked my in front of white castle's right across the street from ST Anthony's. "Carl, I'm proud of you, you too Keisha. Remember you both are baby Christians. Chenille has problems that out of our hands. I'm not in a position to make her problems my problems."

"I was never asking you to Leroy."

"That's why you're going to go inside
ST. Anthony's and pray to God Chenille. Now I'll
walk you inside because you really need to go to the
Lord with your problem and not me. Not Mother
Love, not no flesh period go to God Chenille."

Chenille and I walked outside and across the street
to ST. Anthony's. Chenille and I entered the Church,
I sent Carl and Keisha to get us something to eat
while Chenille and I was going to do some serious
praying for our sins. As we got on our knees
Chenille smiled at me and grabbed my manhood
telling me she was horny and kept smiling.

"Woman, you really need to do some serious
praying." I said moving her hand.

I waited a few more seconds for a response from
Chenille. Instead she look at Jesus on the chrost and
stared at him as if she heard his voice. "Lord forgive
me of my sins and bring my husband to me so we
can be a family."

With that being said I stepped to the side and let
Chenille have her moment. I had my own praying to
do and asking God for forgiveness has relived me
off the stress some of these woman can put a man
through. Even if it's just a friends with benefits
thing. The point is I was not going to be holding
myself accountable for Chenille and her husband's
problems. In fact I was going to take control of this

situation and make sure Chenille go to her husband because dealing with her pregnancy was not my problem. Carl and Keisha came inside the Church with White Castle. With Carl and Keisha here I knew the Church was going to be turned out.

Carl

Although we all were in Church I felt like I was floating on air. We shared a bunch of kisses before, but I'd never kissed a woman like Keisha laid on me at the church and inside Uncle Leroy's car Keisha's lips were so soft and she smelled so good she made every other woman, even the ones I had one night stands with. Keisha made things so easy for us and I have to include God in that happening. We sat in Uncle Leroy's car and were kissing all over one another before heading into

St. Anthony's and then prayed with each other. That what I love about Keisha. We knew not to take it any farther because we would not be leaving Uncle Leroy's car. We quickly headed inside the Church with Uncle Leroy's food. I was enjoying this time with Keisha in the car so much I considered begging her for us not to leave. I hate to admit it, but Keisha had me open and ready to give her a baby. But it would take some serious praying because I was not about to just be any woman's baby father.

Derrick

29

I never loved a woman as much as I did Gabrielle. I never been in a situation like this before either, my fiancée is a former stripper and she used to work for my Uncle Leroy. He swears he always protected her and Keisha and it's just crazy because I now found myself inside Dr. Waves office early Monday morning.

"I don't get it. It's as if I'm being punished. I mean that's what it seems like."

Dr. Wave looked at me as I exhaled and stared at him.

"Why do you say that Derrick?"

"I mean when I was in high school yeah, I'd have 3 or 4 girlfriends and even in college. But since meeting Gab things changed. I mean I've changed even before meeting Gabrielle I changed but to go through his." I said.

"What do you mean changed? Dr. Wave said as he kept taking notes in his pad.

The Doctor just didn't get it he was probably married and got a scholar ship to go to school.

"I mean Dr. Wave, I cut of all ties with those other women and since I dated so many I knew the kind of woman I was looking for."

"REALLY?"

"Yes, I knew the kind of men women wanted at least I thought I did."

"Well she's not for you but, go on."

"There's not really much to say Doc. The more I try to understand women the more confusing they get. But there's 1 thing I learned.

"And what's that?"

I stood up and and looked at Dr. Wave because this is something I'm sure he could agree with me on. "I've learned that each woman what's something different I'm out of here Doc." I said shaking his hand.

I went out received a call from Gabrielle, but I didn't pick it up I just was not ready to talk with anybody. I knew sooner or later I'd have to because Gabrielle is still the mother of my daughter.

Maybe Dr. Wave is right maybe Gabrielle isn't for me. As I was walking toward my moms home I stopped for a moment and said a prayer. 'Dear God, I'm asking for the strength and knowledge and wisdom to dealing with these emotions I'm having about Gabrielle. I'm not sure if we even have a future only you know that God. I'm praying that you watch over my daughter and help me get through this situation Amen.'

I think the stress of finding out about Gabrielle past had really taken a toll on me, but I was ready to tell her I wanted us to be a family again. Our daughter deserved to have both her parents and I was going to let my mm know I had a personal talk with God and that's why the I love my mom. Mother Love is the woman who taught me whenever I have a problem go to God about it. Having a future with Gabrielle is something I'm looking forward too.

Gabrielle

30

I sat down on my couch pouring myself a glass of champagne. I was hoping Derrick would answer his phone things between us just gotten out of hand and I was hoping we can patch things up. Derrick was not answering his phone all day he hadn't seen our daughter in 3 day's. I put my daughter to sleep and drank the bottle of Champagne I made. I looked at a BlackLoveEntertainment magazine and the title of it said. 'Why are most women never satisfied?' Another article in the magazine said.

'The things couples face after having a baby.' I read both articles the 1st one said. Most women get married for the wrong reason. They can say they love their partner, if it's male or female but when things get hard and they will. Will you still be there through the thick and thin times in that marriage? Most women complain that their partner is not paying attention to them enough or that he's not taking care of home the right way. Instead of looking inward at themselves they blame him or her for their problems of not being happy. Then when they get fed up, frustrated, and hurt, some women make the problems in their relationships worst than what it already is by judging and criticizing their partner.

Instead of tackling the issues they want to escalate it. They punish their partner and do it by with holding sex, not being affectionate, and not giving their partner attention. That causes problem in the marriage. Never wanting to admit when your wrong causes problems you'll must learn to tackle the issues you'll are having. If you don't there will be problems after problems after problem and eventually he or she is going to get tired of being your punching bag.

The next article I read the things couples face after a baby. Although every pregnancy is different most women don't realize when the have post pardon depression. They feel like there not cared for, they've go about feeling taken advantage or not feeling heard or seen. They don't feel loved or appreciated enough by their spouse. It happens to the best of women, often these women even the strongest, smartest, most independent of them believe that they can inflict enough pain back onto their partners or do whatever it is to exact enough control of them. Ladies, that's wrong no one should be in a relationship or marriage to control their spouse. Instead try helping them or let them figure out whatever it is on their own. the opposite usually happens. The woman may not feel loved enough by her spouse and she's tired and fed up of feeling nagged, controlled, and criticized do the opposite. I really felt offended for all when especially women of color. Now I understand there are some women who try to use a baby to hurt the man and think their getting even with him. Me I wasn't going to be that type of parent. I called Derrick again but his phone went straight to voicemail. I decided to call my parents and ask them to come watch my little girl.

30 minutes later I went to St. Anthony's Church to see Pastor Sharp and as I was headed inside he was headed outside. "Gabrielle, how are you?" Pastor Sharp asked.

"I'm fine Pastor, I was coming to see you because I have a few question and things to discuss with you."

"Well I was just finishing up with…"

"Dr. Wave, and it's a pleasure to meet such a beautiful woman." Dr. Wave said as he handed me his business card.

Dr. Wave smiled as his eyes traveled up and down at me.

"Gabrielle, I have a family emergency but I have a moment if you want to talk."

"No, no Pastor Sharp if it's an emergency than go. Do what's more important." I said knowing I really needed to talk to him.

"Then if you'll both excuse me." Pastor Sharp said as he walked off.

"Ms. Gabrielle if you're not busy I'd like to take you out to dinner tonight?"

"I'd love that but I have my daughter to take care of."

I was really upset with myself but I really wanted to speak with Pastor Sharp because not hearing from Derrick really bothered me. I really what him to be a part of his daughter's life and not be angry about my pass. I watched Dr. Wave get ready to get in his BMW X7. "Dr. Wave?"

Yes, Ms. Gabrielle what can I do for you."

I just wanted to apologizes, it just that I'm going thought some things."

"We all are. That's why I suggested to take a beautiful woman such as yourself out."

"And I'm going to take you up on your offer. Here's my number. Call me in about 2 hours."

I gave Dr. Wave my number and went home to get ready for our date. It's time I stop being at home waiting for Derrick to come home so we can be a family. As much as I love Derrick, I have to love myself and my little girl even more. Derrick is a good man and all but I'm not about to be waiting on no man at all to show me he wants to be a family.

1 hours and 10 minutes later the doorbell rang. Just a minute I looked at myself in the mirror because this is my first time going out with someone other than Derrick and as I put my lipstick on and was ready to have a good time. I let my parents take my daughter over to their house for the night. As for me I was going out and as I looked at Dr. Wave he had on a grey suit and a bow tie. It didn't matter to me anymore I had to face reality and that I'm now a single parent and I was about to make sure I have a good time tonight. As I opened the door there were flowers right there waiting for me in Dr. Waves hand and as he handed them to me he kissed my hand and I welcomed him with a hug. Dr. Wave is a true gentlemen and if this is what God had instore for me who am I to argue

Group guide for readers
reading, groups,
bookclubs and people who
just love to read.

She's not for you

By

Kasim Power

Questions and discussion
about this book.

1. Who was your favorite character and why?

2. Did you think Derrick was overreacting how would you have handled that situation.

3. What do you think of Rachel?

4. Do you think Mother Love did thing right thing trying to open her brothers eyes.

5. Were you happy with how Mother Love having Church in her home.

6. Are you happy for Uncle Leroy?

7. What was your reaction when Derrick punched Carl? How would you handle that situation.

8. Do you think Keisha and Gabrielle friendship can be like it was before.

9. Would you have done what Mother Love did for everyone?

10. Did Gabrielle make the right choice in going on a date with Dr. Wave?

Here's a look at Kasim next book and to find out about Dr. Wave and his origin read the Novel Pure Evil. The sequel to She's not for you will be in Mother Love says Prayer Changes things. Based on another hit stage play by written, directed, and produced by Kaism Power. Also, you can catch Carl and Uncle Leroy in Caught between women.

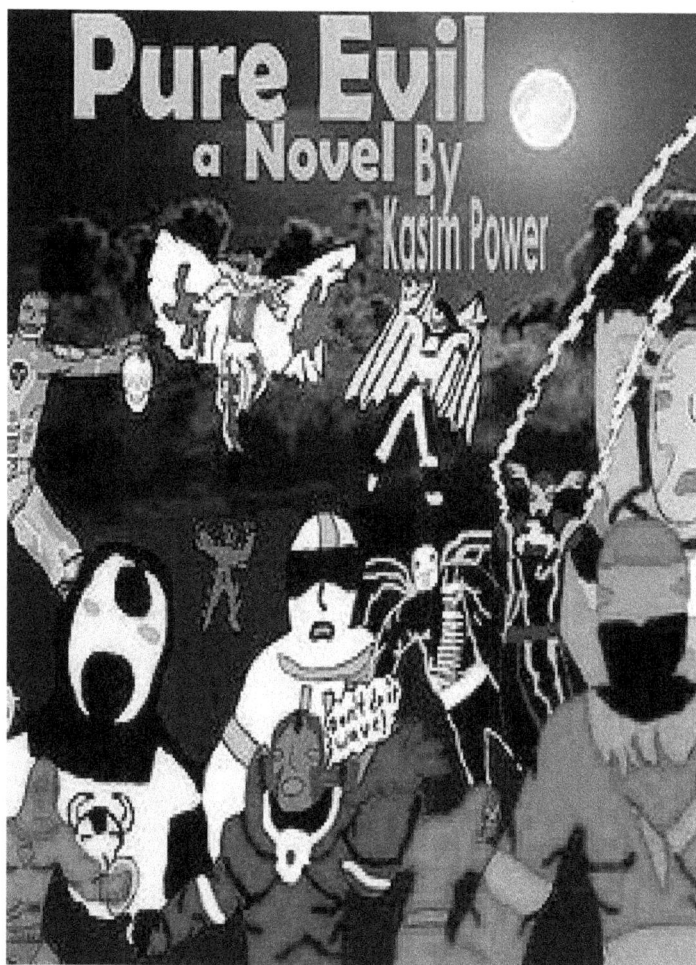

Epilogue

Why me? Why would he choose me to take over this organization? Not to mention looking after his woman. Who I'm now married too and love dearly.

These are the thoughts that were going through my mind as I sat on the roof of the Clock Tower building thinking. All this responsibility I had to deal with and these ego's in this organization. I've dealt with my Wife and son, Gymrat, FirePie, Chaotic, Bloodthrust, Moonstabber, and the one man who has the biggest ego and the most stubborn person I've ever met Dr. Wave. I didn't even mention his personal Bounty Hunter Shadow Shooter.

2 years ago 2015 Empire City aka Brooklyn.

7:00 pm

"I know I'm asking a lot but I know you're the right man for the job."

"And what makes you think that? I'm not smart like Wave, nor do I possess his skills and power.

"Sam."

"You know not to call me that, Anthony."

"Fare enough, ok LiveWire, let me explain this as best as I could. Being a leader isn't always about who's more powerful or who accomplished more in their life."

"What are you talking about Power?"

Yes, don't get it twisted Wave, wasn't all that powerful until he started studying that Witchcraft/ Black Magic and all that other shit. Then all that cockiness came."

"Yeah, I remember, but do you really think I'm the right man for the job?"

"I do! Look LiveWire as I said being a leader is about being effective, because great leaders are born not made. Which is why I want you to take over in my absence and look over Kenna."

But LadyFlames is..."

"Yes, I know she's my girl, but we have a complicated relationship. Look I'm not going to get into that now."

Do you realize what you're asking me?"

I do realize I know you'll help take us to new heights. Because regardless of people's ego's like Dr. Wave, we do have a strong team.

"I can't believe this. Where are you going anyway?" "To train with DNA. Look LiveWire, you'll be fine once you know the values of each individual as well as what they need from you as their leader there's no law you can't break to get the job done."

"Well I already know everyone's overall purpose."

"And that's why I picked you are an effective leader. Here's a lists of Cops, Correction Officers, Judges, and Lawyers and people who've gotten in our way or broken the law and gotten away with it. And when I say the law I mean our law."

"Take care son."

A Black Love Entertainment & Real Creations Event

Caught Between Women

A Novel by Kasim Power